# MYSTERIES, LEGENDS, AND UNEXPLAINED PHENOMENA

## ASTROLOGY AND DIVINATION

# MYSTERIES, LEGENDS, AND UNEXPLAINED PHENOMENA

Astrology and Divination

ESP, Psychokinesis, and Psychics

Ghosts and Haunted Places

UFOs and Aliens

Werewolves

# MYSTERIES, LEGENDS, AND UNEXPLAINED PHENOMENA

# ASTROLOGY AND DIVINATION

**ROBERT M. PLACE**

Consulting Editor: Rosemary Ellen Guiley

CHELSEA HOUSE
PUBLISHERS
An imprint of Infobase Publishing

# ASTROLOGY AND DIVINATION

Chelsea House
An imprint of Infobase Publishing
132 West 31st Street
New York NY 10001

**Library of Congress Cataloging-in-Publication Data**

Place, Robert Michael.
  Astrology and divination / Robert M. Place ; consulting editor, Rosemary Ellen Guiley.
      p. cm.—(Mysteries, legends, and unexplained phenomena)
  Includes bibliographical references and index.
  ISBN-13: 978-0-7910-9385-6 (alk. paper)
  ISBN-10: 0-7910-9385-9 (alk. paper)
  1. Astrology. 2. Divination. I. Guiley, Rosemary. II. Title.
  BF1708.P53 2008
  133.3—dc22  2007038137

Chelsea House books are available at special discounts when purchased in bulk quantities for businesses, associations, institutions, or sales promotions. Please call our Special Sales Department in New York at (212) 967-8800 or (800) 322-8755.

You can find Chelsea House on the World Wide Web at http://www.chelseahouse.com

Text design by James Scotto-Lavino
Cover design by Ben Peterson
Cover illustration by Robert M. Place

The illustrations in Figure 3.1, 4.3, 4.4, 5.3, 7.1, 7.3, 7.4, 7.5, 7.6, 7.7, and 7.8 and Table 5.2 and 7.1 are Copyright © 2008 Robert M. Place

Printed in the United States of America

Bang FOF 10 9 8 7 6 5 4 3 2 1

This book is printed on acid-free paper.

All links and Web addresses were checked and verified to be correct at the time of publication. Because of the dynamic nature of the Web, some addresses and links may have changed since publication and may no longer be valid.

# Contents

Foreword                                          7

Introduction                                      13

  1  Wise Dreams                            21

  2  Confronting the Divine                 31

  3  Give Yourself A Vision                 39

  4  Omens                                  47

  5  Astrology                              61

  6  Divination Games                       81

  7  The Tarot                              95

Timeline                                          113

Glossary                                          117

Endnotes                                          123

Further Resources                                 125

Bibliography                                      127

Index                                             129

About the Author                                  135

About the Consulting Editor                       136

# Foreword

Did you ever have an experience that turned your whole world upside down? Maybe you saw a ghost or a UFO. Perhaps you had an unusual, vivid dream that seemed real. Maybe you suddenly knew that a certain event was going to happen in the future. Or, perhaps you saw a creature or a being that did not fit the description of anything known in the natural world. At first you might have thought your imagination was playing tricks on you. Then, perhaps, you wondered about what you experienced and went looking for an explanation.

Every day and night people have experiences they can't explain. For many people these events are life changing. Their comfort zone of what they can accept as "real" is put to the test. It takes only one such experience for people to question the reality of the mysterious worlds that might exist beyond the one we live in. Perhaps you haven't encountered the unknown, but you have an intense curiosity about it. Either way, by picking up this book you've started an adventure to explore and learn more, and you've come to the right place! The book you hold has been written by a leading expert in the paranormal–someone who understands unusual experiences and who knows the answers to your questions.

As a seeker of knowledge, you have plenty of company. Mythology, folklore, and records of the past show that human beings have had paranormal experiences throughout history. Even prehistoric cave paintings and gravesites indicate that early humans had concepts of the supernatural and of an afterlife. Humans have always sought to understand paranormal experiences and to put them into a frame of reference that makes sense to us in our daily lives. Some of the greatest minds in history have grappled with questions about the paranormal. For example, Greek philosopher Plato pondered the nature of dreams and how we "travel" during them. Isaac Newton was interested in the esoteric study of alchemy, which has magical elements, and St. Thomas Aquinas explored the nature of angels and spirits. Philosopher William James joined organizations dedicated to psychical research, and even the inventor of the light bulb, Thomas Alva Edison, wanted to build a device that could talk to the dead. More recently physicists such as David Bohm, Stephen Hawking, William Tiller, and Michio Kaku have developed ideas that may help explain how and why paranormal phenomena happen, and neuroscience researchers like Michael Persinger have explored the nature of consciousness.

Exactly what is a paranormal experience or phenomenon? "Para" is derived from a Latin term for "beyond." So "paranormal" means "beyond normal," or things that do not fit what we experience through our five senses alone and which do not follow the laws we observe in nature and in science. Paranormal experiences and phenomena run the gamut from the awesome and marvelous, such as angels and miracles, to the downright terrifying, such as vampires and werewolves.

Paranormal experiences have been consistent throughout the ages, but explanations of them have changed as societies, cultures, and technologies have changed. For example, our ancestors were much closer to the invisible realms. In times when life was simpler, they saw, felt, and experienced other realities on a daily basis. When night fell, the darkness was thick and quiet, and it was easier to see unusual things, such as ghosts. They had no electricity to keep the night lit up. They had no media for constant communication and entertainment. Travel was difficult. They had more time to notice subtle things that were just beyond their ordinary senses. Few doubted their experiences. They accepted the invisible realms as an extension of ordinary life.

Today we have many distractions. We are constantly busy from the time we wake up until we go to bed. The world is full of light and noise 24 hours a day, seven days a week. We have television, the

Internet, computer games, and cell phones to keep us busy, busy, busy. We are ruled by technology and science. Yet, we still have paranormal experiences very similar to those of our ancestors. Because these occurrences do not fit neatly into science and technology, many people think they are illusions, and there are plenty of skeptics always ready to debunk the paranormal and reinforce that idea.

In roughly the past 100 years, though, some scientists have studied the paranormal and attempted to find scientific evidence for it. Psychic phenomena have proven difficult to observe and measure according to scientific standards. However, lack of scientific proof does not mean paranormal experiences do not happen. Courageous scientists are still looking for bridges between science and the supernatural.

My personal experiences are behind my lifelong study of the paranormal. Like many children I had invisible playmates when I was very young, and I saw strange lights in the yard and woods that I instinctively knew were the nature spirits who lived there. Children seem to be very open to paranormal phenomena, but their ability to have these experiences often fades away as they become more involved in the outside world, or, perhaps, as adults tell them not to believe in what they experience, that it's only in their imagination. Even when I was very young, I was puzzled that other people would tell me with great authority that I did not experience what I knew I did.

A major reason for my interest in the paranormal is precognitive dreaming experienced by members of my family. Precognition means "fore knowing," or knowing the future. My mother had a lot of psychic experiences, including dreams of future events. As a teen it seemed amazing to me that dreams could show us the future. I was determined to learn more about this and to have such dreams myself. I found books that explained extrasensory perception, the knowing of information beyond the five senses. I learned about dreams and experimented with them. I taught myself to visit distant places in my dreams and to notice details about them that I could later verify in the physical world. I learned how to send people telepathic messages in dreams and how to receive messages in dreams. Every night became an exciting adventure.

Those interests led me to other areas of the paranormal. Pretty soon I was engrossed in studying all kinds of topics. I learned different techniques for divination, including the Tarot. I learned how to meditate. I took courses to develop my own psychic skills, and I gave psychic readings to others. Everyone has at least some natural psychic ability and can improve it with attention and practice.

Next I turned my attention to the skies, to ufology, and what might be "out there" in space. I studied the lore of angels and fairies. I delved into the dark shadowy realm of demons and monsters. I learned the principles of real magic and spell casting. I undertook investigations of haunted places. I learned how to see auras and do energy healing. I even participated in some formal scientific laboratory experiments for telepathy.

My studies led me to have many kinds of experiences that have enriched my understanding of the paranormal. I cannot say that I can prove anything in scientific terms. It may be some time yet before science and the paranormal stop flirting with each other and really get together. Meanwhile, we can still learn a great deal from our personal experiences. At the very least, our paranormal experiences contribute to our inner wisdom. I encourage others to do the same as I do. Look first for natural explanations of strange phenomena. If natural explanations cannot be found or seem unlikely, consider paranormal explanations. Many paranormal experiences fall into a vague area, where although a natural cause might exist, we simply don't know what could explain them. In that case I tell people to trust their intuition that they had a paranormal experience. Sometimes the explanation makes itself known later on.

I have concluded from my studies and experiences that invisible dimensions are layered upon our world, and that many paranormal experiences occur when there are openings between worlds. The doorways often open at unexpected times. You take a trip, visit a haunted place, or have a strange dream–and suddenly reality shifts. You get a glimpse behind the curtain that separates the ordinary from the extraordinary.

The books in this series will introduce you to these exciting and mysterious subjects. You'll learn many things that will astonish you. You'll be given lots of tips for how to explore the paranormal on your own. Paranormal investigation is a popular field, and you don't have to be a scientist or a full-time researcher to explore it. There are many things you can do in your free time. The knowledge you gain from these books will help prepare you for any unusual and unexpected experiences.

As you go deeper into your study of the paranormal, you may come up with new ideas for explanations. That's one of the appealing aspects of paranormal investigation–there is always room for bold ideas. So, keep an open and curious mind, and think big. Mysterious worlds are waiting for you!

—Rosemary Ellen Guiley

# Introduction

Can we see into the future to tell if we are going to be happy and rich or miserable and poor? What does fate have in store for us? How long will we live? These are the kinds of misguided questions that many people think of when they think of **divination**. Because people think this is what divination is all about, they may think that it is unscientific or, worse, superstitious and just plain dumb. But, divination is not an effort to predict a fated and unchangeable future. If this were true, then divination would not have been respected as it has been throughout most of recorded history. It would not have been respected by the greatest minds of the ancient world, such as Socrates, Sophocles, and Alexander the Great, or played the role it did in the formation of our political, philosophical, and religious history. It is better to label the superstitious effort to predict fate "fortune telling." As we will see, divination is something else.

At its best divination is and always has been the practice of looking to one's inner wisdom for guidance. Cards, star charts, bones, or **crystal balls** are all just tools designed to help us find this inner wisdom. At times divination may point out what is likely to happen in the future but its main concern is to provide insight and guidance that helps one create the future. Don't you wish, sometimes, that you knew a wise seer, someone who knew a lot and had insight into how things work, and that this friend was always available to help when you needed to make important decisions? Well, that is how divination works. It is a way of contacting part of the human mind that lives in the **unconscious** and has greater perspective and access to psychic abilities. It is the oldest and wisest part of one's mind. The ancient Greeks, Romans, and Hebrews, who are the founders of Western culture, believed that this instruction came from the gods or from God and that is why the word divination was formed to describe it. The word literally means to get in touch with the divine. It is derived from the Latin *deus*, meaning god. In modern terminology, this source of wisdom may be referred to as the **Higher Self** or Wiser Self.

## A WORD FROM CARL G. JUNG

If you are not, however, convinced that a physical object like a deck of cards or the planets orbiting around the sun can have anything to do with you and your life, look at the exploration of this process by one of the greatest minds of the twentieth century, the famous Swiss psychiatrist Carl G. Jung (1875-1961). Jung and other psychiatrists who worked with dreams and explored the unconscious part of the human mind observed incidents with their patients that they described as predictions, **telepathy**, or **clairvoyance**. That means in their dreams these patients saw what was likely to happen the next day, knew what someone was thinking without speaking to them, or knew details about something that should have been hidden from them. Jung also noticed that such things happened to himself, his colleagues, and members of his family.

Jung concluded that if anyone looked objectively into his findings and the findings of other psychologists, they would see that these telepathic abilities were undeniably real.[1] He also believed they showed that the human mind did not seem to be limited by time and space. In other words for a person to know the future or to know things that he could not physically see or touch meant that his mind was not confined in the body but existed beyond it. In the modern world most people have become accustomed to thinking of our minds as living in our brains, but Jung was saying that the brain works something like a television set and the mind is like the signals that it picks up. Just like it would be silly to believe that actors on television are living inside the set, we should not think that our thoughts and feelings are just in the brain. Not being confined by time or space, the mind is capable of connecting with the minds of other people far away and because the connections are outside of time they happen instantly. Also, because the mind is not restricted by time it can look at where we are likely to be in the future.

Besides observing these things happening in dreams, Jung also noticed that seemingly magical coincidences happened in everyday life. For example, Jung was talking to his patient about the symbolism of the Egyptian scarab

**Figure 0.1**   *Swiss psychologist Carl Gustav Jung smoking a pipe in 1961.* (Bettmann/Corbis)

beetle while he was looking out the window of his office and at that exact moment a large beetle walked across the glass in front of him, as if it had arrived just to illustrate his discussion. Ancient peoples would consider such an event a message from the gods, or an "omen." Jung decided to create a new term for these events, one that sounded more scientific. He called them examples of **synchronicity**, combining *syn*, which means together, with *chron*, which means time. Then Jung tacked *icity* on the end to make it into a noun, so that it would be a thing that could be studied.

Jung defines synchronicity as an event happening in the physical world that coincides with an event happening in our minds, together in time, in a way that the mind feels it is meaningful, like a message from the gods or God. Nothing specific causes this to happen; it just occurs because the outer world of physical reality and the inner world of the mind are connected. Jung also found that each moment in time had its own quality and certain things seemed to happen together. Once Jung created this term he was able to study synchronicity as a part of psychology and he realized that synchronicity was also at work when people did divination. He started looking into **astrology** and spent a lot of time studying an ancient Chinese book used for divination called the *I Ching* (pronounced "EE jing").

There is another important term that Jung used in his study: unconscious. The conscious part of our mind is what we are thinking, feeling, and noticing right now. The unconscious part is *not conscious*. Normally people use this word to describe someone who is knocked out or asleep. When we sleep our minds are still working but they work differently; they create dreams. Dreams have a different logic about them than reality does when we are awake and things can happen in this unconscious realm that cannot take place in conscious reality. For example, we might see ourselves flying or we could suddenly be in a distant location. What Jung and other psychiatrists discovered is that this not-conscious part of the mind communicates with symbols instead of words. Symbols are images and sounds that have meanings that cannot always be put into words. Psychiatrists also discovered that this process is always going on in our minds, even when we are awake, just outside the focus of our conscious mind, and dreams are just the surface of something even larger.

Have you ever wondered where your thoughts or memories come from? Neuroscientists have observed how the brain functions while memories are being stored or retrieved. They have come up with theories about which parts of the brain are being activated and how neural connections form. They have also classified different types of memories, such as short term and long term. But, as Jung said, the mind is not confined by the physical. In Jung's view, neuroscientists are like technicians observing the workings of a television set but unable to tell us much about the actors on the shows. The essence of thoughts and memories is still a mystery.

You do not need to be a neuroscientist to explore the mystery of thought. You can do it right now. Hopefully, at present, you are thinking about what you are reading, but if you try to remember something that happened earlier today, that memory would suddenly come into your mind from someplace else. You were not conscious of it and now you are. Where did it come from? If we sit quietly with our eyes closed and observe our thoughts, we can see that they keep coming out of that same other-place. If we go deeper into a relaxed state, as we do in meditation, we will begin to see dream-like images, but these too are coming from someplace else. No matter how deep we go, we will always see that these thoughts or symbols are coming from somewhere deeper. That deeper place is the unconscious, and Jung realized that it was much bigger than the conscious part of the mind. The experience that he had was like the one we have when we look at the stars at night and realize how big the universe is. Jung found that the unconscious is as big as the physical universe. And, it's all inside us.

As Jung explored this vast inner universe, he discovered that we all have other, very different personalities inside of us and that these personalities fit certain patterns that are the same in all people. In various mythologies, religions, and folk beliefs around the world, Jung saw that these inner personalities took the form of various heroes, gods, angels, and demons. Although these characters all wore different clothes, had different names, and spoke different languages, they had more important things in common that showed that they were all forms of the same inner personalities. For example, we can see that there are ancient goddesses associated with the moon, like Artemis in Greece, Diana in Rome, and Isis in Egypt. All of these goddesses have certain things in common. They are beautiful, protective of women, and associated with childbirth. When the ancient religions that worshiped these goddesses disappeared, the qualities that they represented did not. We can find these same things associated with modern religious figures, such as Saint Mary, who is associated with beauty, motherhood, and the moon in Christianity and the Bodhisattva Quan Yin, who is associated with the same things in Buddhism. Jung called these inner people the **archetypes** (pronounced "AR-ka-types"). And, just as the archetypes could appear in myths and visions, personal versions could also be found in dreams.

Jung believed that these archetypes, which are the same in all people, come from a deep part of the unconscious where the minds of all people are connected. He called this the collective unconscious. So, if our minds are all connected, we can all share thoughts and ideas. The trick is to get this insight out of the not-conscious part of the mind and into the part that is conscious. That is where divination comes in. Besides all of these archetypes, like mothers, fathers, teachers, lovers, heroes, and monsters, Jung found that there was one central archetype that was bigger and deeper and connected to all of the others. He called this archetype the Self. This is the same as the Higher Self, mentioned above, but Jung just called it the Self. The Self is the whole mind, bigger than its parts, and it is the place where the conscious, the unconscious, and the collective unconscious minds connect. So, the object of divination is to communicate with this Self or Higher Self and let the conscious mind make use of all its wisdom and knowledge.

## THREE TYPES OF DIVINATION

Since before the beginning of history people around the world have sought out help from intuitively gifted men and women who could guide them to inner wisdom. In tribal cultures these gifted diviners are called shamans, and their methods include the interpretation of dreams, visions, and signs from the natural world called omens, and the interpretation of natural patterns, such as the pattern of bones or sticks thrown onto the ground. As the first civilizations appeared these shamans became priests and prophets and their forms of divination evolved. The Babylonian priests, looking to the sky for omens, developed astrology; the Hebrew prophets, looking into their dreams and visions for the word of God, wrote religious texts; and the ancient Greek **oracles** went into a trance, spoke for a god, and from their words wise men like Socrates developed philosophy. Along with these shamans, priests, prophets, and oracles, ordinary people also sought ways to get to this advice. They made use of astrology and books, but

## Jung's Image of the Self

Although Jung found that the archetype of the Self could appear in dreams as a circular diagram, a rock, a giant figure, the center of a landscape, or other things, perhaps one of its most useful appearances was as a wise teacher. Jung discovered this in his own dreams in 1914 when a wise teacher in the form of an old man with a beard and large wings like a kingfisher bird flew into his dream. Jung named him Philemon, and he became a regular figure in his dreams and fantasies, one he was able to talk with and learn things from. What clued Jung in as to why this Philemon would be important to him was a synchronistic event connected with the first dream.

After Jung first dreamed of Philemon he realized he was onto something, and over the next few days he painted Philemon's picture with a white beard, a long, colorful sort of ancient robe, a golden halo, and large green, red, and black kingfisher wings. While Jung was working on the painting, he decided to take a break and walked out into his garden to the shore of the lake where he lived. On the shore he found a dead kingfisher. Now, these birds are rare where Jung lived, he had never seen one on his property before, and he never saw one again. As you can imagine, he was blown away. Jung realized that this was an example of synchronicity. He further realized that there was a connection between synchronicity and the archetypes and that this showed that there was a connection between our inner mental world and the outer physical world.[2]

also everyday objects like dice and cards. They helped themselves and each other and this practice continues to this day.

This book is an overview of the history and forms of divination that have existed in human culture around the world from prehistoric times to the present. Although they were all trying to communicate with the same deep part of the unconscious, people around the world have used many methods of divination from ancient shamans using rocks and bones to modern diviners using very artistic looking **Tarot** cards and mathematically accurate astrology charts. To help organize this material, the forms of divination are divided into three categories based on how people tried to connect with the Higher Self. They are

- **Intuitive Divination**: The direct connection with the Higher Self through dreams or an oracle or a prophet. An oracle or a prophet is someone gifted at contacting the Higher Self through visions. This form of divination is covered in Chapters One through Three.

- **Inductive Divination**: Looking for signs of the communication with the Higher Self in nature, such as omens. This led to the practice of astrology and palmistry. This is discussed in Chapters Four and Five.

- **Interpretative Divination**: Connecting with the Higher Self through the use of random patterns, created by human interaction with objects such as stones, sticks, bones, coins, or dice. This led to the creation of Tarot cards and the Chinese divinatory book the *I Ching*. This is explored in Chapters Six through Eight.

# Wise Dreams

One morning in the early 1400s in the town of Swaffham, in Norfolk County, England, a poor tinker named John Chapman woke up from a dream, and told his wife that instead of mending pots, which is what he usually did for money, he was going to walk to the city of London that day and stand on a bridge that he saw in his dream.

"Why in the world would you do that?" his wife said.

"Well," replied John, "in my dream, I saw that if I stood on a certain spot on London Bridge I would meet a man who would tell me something of great importance."

"What?" his wife asked.

"I don't know," said John, "but it would be good to go and find out."

"Are you a fool?" she replied, "Go to work!"

John did start feeling foolish, so, he picked up his hammer and went to work at his bench, while his wife prepared breakfast. The next night, however, and the night after that he had the same dream. After the third time John and his wife were convinced that there was something to these dreams. John got ready that morning and walked to London and stood on his dream spot, but nothing happened for the rest of the day.

John thought to himself, *Well this isn't good; if I go back now I will really look foolish.* So, he found a place to stay for the night, went back to the bridge the next morning, and stood. Nothing happened the second day either but John came back a third day. Toward evening as John was beginning to get discouraged, a London shopkeeper came up and asked why John had been standing there all this time. John told him about the dreams.

The shopkeeper laughed and said, "I never pay attention to dreams. They are all nonsense. Just the other night I had a silly dream about a box of money buried under an oak tree next to a tinker's shop in a place called Swaffham. What a joke," he said, while walking away.

John walked away also, right back to Swaffham, and to the garden next to his shop with its big oak tree. After digging for a while, the next day, he found a metal box filled with coins. "Besides the coins the box had an inscription written in Latin. John had to find a scribe to read it for him but what it said made him even more excited. The inscription said that there was more and richer treasure yet to be found if he dug a little deeper. Early the following morning John discovered another box under the oak tree. This one was filled with gold and silver. Now, John and his wife were rich.

Although John's story has been preserved as a folk story with several variations in the details, John Chapman's tombstone can be found in the Swaffham cemetery and the town records show that, although he was a tinker, in 1454 he had enough money to fund the building of a church.[3] This fact suggests that there is some truth behind this legend. So, don't be afraid to follow your dream.

## DREAM DIVINATION

People spend about one-third of their lives sleeping. In the last 10 years, therefore, you were probably asleep three years and four months. When you are asleep you are naturally communicating with the unconscious part of your mind, where the archetypes live. Your dreams are this type of communication. The ability to dream is believed to have evolved in mammals about 130 million years ago.

Like all mammals, such as dogs, cats, and cows, humans dream and have always dreamed as long as they have been around. It is not surprising, therefore, that dreams are the oldest and most natural form of divination. All you have to do to participate is fall asleep. This form of divination is called **oneiromancy**, which is derived from the Greek word for dream, *oneiros*, combined with the Greek word for **prophecy**, *manteia*.

Tribal people around the world find a rich source of artistic, cultural, and spiritual inspiration in their dreams and look to their dreams as a way of obtaining direction and advice. Judging from their

**Figure 1.1**  *An Assyrian cuneiform tablet from a merchant colony. It was created between 1900 and 1800 BC.*  (Christie's Images/Corbis)

practices, it seems likely that our prehistoric ancestors were probably heavily involved in dreams in the same ways. Some of the oldest written accounts of dreams are found in the Epic of Gilgamesh, a story that is one the first things ever written and is written in one of the oldest known forms of writing, cuneiform, which looks like little triangles pressed into a clay tablet. Gilgamesh is an ancient Sumerian hero who is thought to have lived in the third millennium BCE. The ancient Sumerians, Assyrians, and Babylonians all wrote about his mythic adventures fighting monsters and avoiding floods. These are people who lived in "the cradle of civilization" between the Tigris and Euphrates Rivers, a region that scholars refer to by its ancient Greek name, Mesopotamia, and which includes modern Iraq, and parts of Syria, Iran, and Turkey. Gilgamesh was to them like Hercules was to the Greeks. Through all of his adventures Gilgamesh looked for

## The First Known Dream

The first actual historic person we know of who had his dream written down was the Sumerian king Gudea, who was dreaming sometime around 2200 BCE. Gudea wanted to build a temple to the god Ningirsu, a god of rain and fertility, and the god sent him a confusing dream of a winged giant with two lions and a donkey digging the ground with its hoof. Gudea needed to call in an expert to interpret the dream, so he prayed to Gatumdug, the local mother goddess, for help. Gatumdug told him that the winged giant was Ningirsu and he, Gudea, was the donkey in his dream. She told him, further, that his impatient digging showed that he was being impatient with this temple project. It is a good thing that he got this answer from a goddess and not somebody he could have had killed for giving him unwelcome news.

direction in his dreams. It seems that he couldn't do anything without sleeping on it first. Gilgamesh would try to interpret his dreams by looking for omens in them to get an idea about what he was headed for in the future. So, if he dreamed about the heavens roaring with lightning and the earth trembling he figured that something bad was going to happen to someone. Generally, Gilgamesh's good luck depended on the correct interpretation of his dreams and the misinterpretation of dreams brought bad luck. Occasionally, however, a god would show up in his dreams and make things simple by just giving him advice.

## DREAM BOOKS

Because the people of Mesopotamia valued their dreams as a source of omens, they began to write lists of the stuff you could expect to find in dreams and what each thing meant. These were the first **dream books**. It would seem that these books might be useful to us now in translation but they do not seem to work for modern people. Interpretations of things in dreams depend on familiar characters from stories, similar cultural references, and words that sound alike but mean different things, called puns. Because we do not hear the same stories and speak the same language as the ancient Mesopotamians, most of their suggested meanings make little sense to us.

Dream books, however, do seem to work some of the time when used within the culture that they are meant for and most ancient cultures had them. The Egyptians had collections of dream books, starting from 2050 to 1790 BCE, that were written on papyrus, a type of paper that they made out of grassy stalks. The Chinese had *Chou Kung's Book of Auspicious and Inauspicious Dreams*, written about 1020 BCE. Chou Kung also worked on the *I Ching*. In India part of the Vedas, which is like the Bible to Hindus, written between 1500 and 1000 BCE, is actually a dream book listing lucky and unlucky dreams. The Greeks and Romans also had dream books dating from the fifth century BCE.

Being that the Vedas are similar to a bible, it's fair to wonder if the Old Testament in the Bible, written from about 1500 to 400 BCE, also contains a dream book. It does not, but it certainly attests to the ancient Hebrews belief in the importance of dream divination. The diviners in the Bible are called prophets and the entire text is an account of their announcements and predictions that come to them from God. How does God speak to the prophets? Well, God clearly states in the Bible "If anyone among you is a prophet I will make myself known to him in a vision, I will speak to him in a dream." (Numbers 12:6)

Besides inspiring the prophets through dreams, God also gave the ancient Hebrews the ability to interpret the dreams of other people. The Bible tells us that while the Hebrew people were held captive in Babylon the prophet Daniel had a chance to interpret the dream of the Babylonian king, Nebuchadnezzar (605-562 BCE). He is the king who built the famous Hanging Gardens, which were one of the wonders of the ancient world. The king dreamed that he saw a huge statue with a golden head, a silver chest, a belly of brass, legs of iron, and one foot of clay. The king threatened to kill the prophet if he failed to interpret the dream, but Daniel was not worried because God told him what to say. He said that the golden head represented Nebuchadnezzar's rule, but he predicted that the lesser metals represented a gradual decline in the status of the kingdom during the reigns for the rulers to come. The king seemed to like the interpretation because he didn't kill Daniel, and later he allowed him to interpret another dream about a giant tree.

In a similar incident the prophet Joseph, who while in prison in Egypt interpreted the dreams of other inmates, was called on to interpret the pharaoh's dream. The pharaoh, which was the title of the king in Egypt, dreamed of seven fat cows and seven lean cows. Joseph told him that the dream was a prediction that there would be seven years of prosperity followed by seven years of failing crops and lack of food. Not being one to give into fate, Joseph suggested that they save enough from the years of plenty to cover their needs in the lean years. The grateful pharaoh put Joseph in charge of this project.

The early Christians thought about dreams in two ways. They saw dreams as an important way to communicate with God, which was good, but they also believed that some dreams were derived from sinful desires, which was bad. This, however, did not stop them from writing dream books. The most popular book, and one of the best, was written by Synesius of Cyrene (373-414 CE), a Greek Christian and the bishop of Ptolemais in Libya. Besides the benefits of divination, Synesius believed that communicating with your spirit through dreams just felt really good.

From the Middle Ages to the modern world there have been many different opinions about the value of dreams, as we saw in John Chapman's story at the beginning of the chapter. In the Islamic world, because Mohammad was inspired by his dreams, dreams have always been valued. In the Christian world, some mystics were great believers in the power of dreams while other church leaders worried that dreams could just as easily come from the devil as from God. One of the first Christians to suggest this was Tertullian (155-230 CE), who was a priest in Rome and wrote on dreams in his *Treatise on the Soul*. Although Tertullian believed that some dreams could come from the devil he did not think that they were necessarily harmful. Some later Christians were not so understanding. Martin Luther (1483-1546), the founder of Lutheranism, for example, was so upset about trying to figure out which dreams were from God and which from the devil that he decided it was better to just not pay attention to his dreams at all.[4] Yet most Christian mystics, artists, writers, and philosophers continued to value dreams as a source of wisdom.

In the 1700s, the Age of Enlightenment, when the Western world wholeheartedly adopted a scientific attitude, dreams were demoted to a scientific curiosity and tended to be dismissed. In the twentieth century, Austrian psychiatrist Sigmund Freud (1856-1939), the father of psychoanalysis, looked to dreams as a door to the unconscious and

## Dream Incubation

Dream divination sounds like a good idea but suppose you need to know about something specific. Do you have to just wait and see if you get a dream about it? Ancient people asked themselves the same question and developed a way of giving themselves a dream that answers a specific question. This is called dream **incubation**.

In the ancient world incubation was mostly practiced in temples. A ritual prepared the dreamer to ask the god of the temple for a dream in answer to his or her question, and then the person would sleep in the temple that night. Dream incubation was practiced by most of the ancient cultures discussed in this chapter.

Perhaps the most highly developed form of dream incubation was that of the ancient Greeks, who practiced in temples dedicated to Asclepius, the god of medicine and healing. The dreamer was usually someone who was sick and wanted to know how to recover. The dreamer would be instructed to fast and bathe daily to prepare for the event. On the day of the incubation a ram would be sacrificed and the dreamer would lie on its skin on an altar in the temple below the statue of the god. The floor of the temple was crawling with snakes, because Asclepius liked them and they were a symbol of healing. Then hymns were sung, lamps were lit, and the dreamer would ask Asclepius to send him or her a dream with a cure. In the morning the priests would help the dreamer interpret the dream and start working on the cure.[5]

You can work on dream incubation yourself, without the temple and snakes, right in your bedroom. Before you go to bed just ask your Higher Self to send you a dream with the answer to your question. Or, you can write your question on a piece of paper before you go to bed, place it under your pillow, and sleep on it. Be sure to keep a pad and pencil next to your bed so that you can write your dream down in the morning. That is the best way to remember it.

revived interest in them. Freud tended to look at dreams as coming from nasty impulses in the unconscious. One of Freud's students, Carl G. Jung, later broke away from his teacher to explore dreams on his own as a source of wisdom. He discovered that they could be a source of predictions, telepathic information, and other insights. Thanks to Jung and other researchers like him, people are interested in dream divination today.

# Confronting the Divine

This was Hippalus' first visit to the oracle of Apollo at Delphi. By sunset he had ascended Mount Parnassos. There, nestled at the top beneath the twin cliffs, glowing red with the sun's last rays, was a magnificent complex of statues and Doric-style buildings, including the main temple or sanctuary. Hippalus' father was a merchant and he wanted to know if a voyage would be prosperous at this time. He would not think of launching this voyage without the approval of Apollo and he provided his son with plenty of gold coins to pay for his stay in the inn and to pay the consultation tax, called the *palanos*.

On the morning of the seventh day after the new moon, a number sacred to Apollo, Hippalus purified himself in a ritual bath in the Castalian Spring. Then, dressed again in his best tunic and a crown of laurel leaves, he joined a group of men and ascended the flagstone steps known as the Sacred Way. At the top they formed a circle outside the temple where a fire blazed on a great stone altar designed to accept sacrifices to the god. Because it was a regular consultation day, the temple priests provided the goat for the sacrifice. The priests sprinkled the animal with holy water, causing it to give an affirmative nod, which was interpreted as a sign of approval so the ritual could continue. After the prayers and offerings the questioners were led by a group of priests and other officials into the first chamber of the temple. Some of the priests were called the *prophetai*, the origin of the word *prophet*, but they were not actually the ones who would receive the visions from the god. Their job was to interpret the visions and utterances of the prophetess called the ***pythia***. It was she who would actually listen to the god.

At the entrance to the inner sanctuary, or *adytum*, the men chose **lots** (numbered stones) to determine their order of entry and, therefore, the order in which their questions would be answered. The men could not see what stone they were choosing and while it may seem

**Figure 2.1** *Greek red-figure painting of King Aigeus consulting the priestess Pythia at Delphi.* (Bettmann/Corbis)

that the order was created by luck, to Hippalus and the other participants it was yet another way of determining the will of Apollo. As Hippalus stepped down into the adytum, he detected a faint sweetness in the air. This was gas coming from deep within the earth under Mount Parnassos. The participants saw it as a sign that the god was present and that the prophesizing could begin. Hippalus sat on a stone bench along the wall with the other participants. From this location they would be able to hear the prophecy but a screen separated them from a view of the three-legged stool, which was the seat of the pythia.

The name of the prophetess, the pythia, was derived from python, the name of a huge dragon or serpent, which in ancient times was believed to have guarded the sanctuary. At that time the sanctuary belonged to the earth goddess Gaia and the dragon was hers. It was said that when Apollo took control of the oracle he slew the python, which blocked his way, and cast its lifeless body into a fissure in the earth found within the temple. The fumes from the decaying body of the python were said to give the inner temple its sweet smell and were responsible for inducing the pythia's prophetic trance. In honor of his victory, Apollo was given the title *pythios*, all things Delphic were referred to as *pythian*, and the prophetess was called the *pythia*.

The pythia was a tall woman in her 50s. Holding a laurel branch and a bowl of holy water, she stepped down into the chamber and climbed onto the high, three-legged stool that stood over the fissure in the floor. As the sweet smelling gas poured over her body she fell into a deep trance. She could see Apollo beckoning her through a mist and sending her meaningful pictures in answer to the questions that the participants asked.

## WHAT HISTORY HAS TO SAY

Today some people think of divination as something only gullible people are interested in but in the ancient world there were numerous oracles that were highly respected by many people, including Socrates, who was considered one of the wisest philosophers of ancient Greece. For a thousand years the oracle at Delphi was the

## It Pays to Ask Twice

It may seem that because the oracle of Delphi was considered to be speaking the word of the god Apollo that questioners would accept their fate and depart once the oracle had spoken. Yet, such blind acceptance of fate is only found in the ancient myths. Ancient historic accounts show that visitors were actually encouraged to question the oracle further and work on a solution to a problem. The oracle was not there to scold them and tell them what bad things were going to happen to them but to help them find solutions to their problems. Here is an example.

In the fifth century BCE the Persians wished to conquer Greece but the Athenian army continued to be the one thing stopping them. In 480 BCE the emperor of Persia, Xerxes (r. 485-465 BCE), sent a massive army to Greece with the intent of destroying Athens. The frightened Athenians sent a runner to the oracle of Delphi to ask the god what to do. The oracle said, "Why sit you doomed one? Fly to the ends of the earth. All is ruin for fire and headlong the god of war shall bring you low." This seemed like the worst pronouncement the oracle could make and, if the Athenians were the kind of people who surrendered to fate, they would have abandoned their city at that time and probably disappeared from history. Themistocles (524-459 BCE), one of Athens's greatest generals, was not satisfied with this answer. He demanded that they send another messenger to Delphi and ask how they could stop the Persians. In response to the second question, the oracle said, "Though all else shall be taken, Zeus, the all seeing, grants that the wooden wall shall not fail."

Themistocles believed that the wooden wall that Zeus referred to was the fleet of ships that he had encouraged the Athenians to build. These

most respected in ancient Greece. Anyone could consult the oracle, from common farmers to kings to ambassadors representing the city-states. Some of the famous men who consulted the oracle were

**Figure 2.2** *A modern replica of a trireme.* (AAAC/Topham/The Image Works)

sleek fast warships, called *triremes*, each had 170 oarsmen on three tiers and a large bronze point on the bow designed to ram and sink an enemy ship. As the Persians approached, the people of Athens abandoned the city and the Persians entered without a fight. The entire Athenian army then manned the fleet of triremes, which they sailed into the narrow strait at Salamis, the body of water between the island of Salamis and the Athenian cost. In the narrow strait they outmaneuvered the bulky Persian ships and sank every one. Without ships to bring supplies, the Persian army had to retreat and the Athenians achieved one of the greatest victories of ancient times. The city of Athens became home to some of the greatest artists and philosophers ever known.[9]

Socrates (470-399 BCE), Sophocles (495-406 BCE), Alexander the Great (356-323 BCE), and Croesus of Lydia (595-546 BCE). Sophocles, a fifth century BCE playwright, wrote that a challenge to the oracle's authority was a challenge to religion itself. To the Greeks, the fact that Apollo was willing to talk to the people through the oracle was the proof of his existence.

In myth the oracle originally belonged to the earth goddess, Gaia, or, in some accounts, the goddess of justice, Themis, and the oracle and was taken over by Apollo at a later date. However, historians say that the oracle was dedicated to Apollo, the god of light, logic, art, and music, from its origin at the end of the ninth century BCE until 393 CE, when it was closed by the Christian emperor Theodosius. As the god of the sun and light, Apollo brought forth clarity and understanding and always spoke the truth. The python, the dragon that was slain by Apollo, was a symbol of the darkness that blocked the light and therefore stopped the messages from getting to the people at Delphi. By killing the python, Apollo allowed his light to shine through and allowed the people to hear the oracle.[6]

Although ancient writers wrote more about the oracle than most subjects, many of the details of the worship and practice at Delphi are still disputed by modern scholars. For example, the first French archeologists who examined the remains of the temple in the 1800s found no evidence of the fissure and the escaping gas that the ancient writers mention. By the middle of the 1900s, most scholars believed that the gas was an invention of the writers and not based on fact. Modern archeologists examining the site, however, have found a fissure in the sanctuary that emits ethylene gas. Ethylene has the potential to cause visions if enough gas is breathed in.[7] Therefore, the modern discovery shows that the ancient writings may be true. Some of the details in the account that opens this chapter may be disputed by some scholars but it is one plausible version of what is likely to have happened on a consultation day at the oracle at the height of its operation in the fifth century BCE.

## OTHER ANCIENT ORACLES

An oracle is basically a person who is gifted at communicating with a god and can help people to ask the god questions and get answers. This ability was probably developed by ancient shamans and similar practices existed among the tribal people of Africa and among the pre-Christian Germanic and Scandinavian tribes. The Greek oracles seem to have been influenced by earlier Egyptian oracles, who were women from important families and spoke for the goddesses Hathor or Neith. Babylonian priestesses were oracles who spoke for the goddess Ishtar. Among the Hebrew people, priests served the same function, only as the spokesmen for Jehovah. Because they were spokesmen for God, the Hebrew prophets can also be considered oracles. According to the ancient Greek historian Herodotus (484-425 BCE), there were 11 oracles in Greece all dedicated to different gods. The ancient Greeks believed that the gods wanted to talk to the people and the oracles were one of the main ways that happened. Besides these 11 oracles, there were more than 400 temples dedicated to Asclepius that also served as oracles. Although one could ask any question of Asclepius, the most common question asked was: "How can I cure this illness?" It was usually answered through dream divination.

In Dodona at the oracle of Zeus, the king of the gods, modern archeologists have dug up a stash of lead tablets on which ancient people wrote the questions that they wanted the god to answer. Among the questions asked were whether a proposed marriage, a trip, or a change of career were wise decisions; whether a wife would have a baby; and how to cure a health problem. But the most popular question was, "How can one keep the favor of the god?"[8] Most modern historians claim that the oracles were used for making predictions but it is interesting that most of these questions asked for advice not predictions.

In the fourth century, as Christianity became the official religion of the Roman world, the pre-Christian oracles began to close down. As a result it is difficult to find an oracle in the modern world. There are, however, some ways people can act as their own oracle. Some people use a Ouija board, which is a board or table top with the words *yes* and *no*, the alphabet, and the numbers zero through nine printed on it. Two people sit with their hands lightly resting on a small pointer, called a *planchette*, which is supported on stilts so that it will glide over the table. As the spirit directs them, the pair will let the pointer move over the board to answer their questions by spelling out words, pointing to numbers, or indicating yes or no. Although this modern tool stems from European tradition, the oldest known oracle table or board like this is the *fuji* created in China in 1200 BCE.

Another more direct way of creating a personal oracle is called **automatic writing**. Simply sit with a pen resting on a pad of paper, write whatever pops into your mind, and keep going. You may be surprised by what your unconscious has to say.

# Give Yourself A Vision

Mary sat in her office alone one evening, wondering what to do about her career. As she often did when she wanted an intuitive answer, she took her crystal ball off the shelf and placed it in front of her on the desk. Her ball was a two-and-a-half-inch wide sphere cut from quartz, a rock that is clear and transparent like glass. The crystal was held about six inches above the desk by a bronze sculpture of Silenus, who was the mythic companion and teacher of Dionysus, the Greek god of wine. Although Silenus, with his fat belly, beard, and horse's ears, was always drunk on wine, he was very wise and gifted at divination. To the ancient Greeks he was like a god of divination.

To avoid any distracting reflections, Mary laid a black silk kerchief flat on her desk and placed Silenus holding the ball in the center of the rectangle. Then, she lit a white candle and turned out the other lights. Mary calmed herself and sat looking at the blank grayish area in the center of her crystal. This was the hard part, but she knew from past experience that all she had to do was sit and wait for something to appear. A few minutes later the space was still blank, but she calmed herself again and kept looking. Then it happened. She began to see a vision that was something like a dream but she was awake and could interact with the characters in this dream. She saw herself on a horse leading a group of men and women toward a sunrise. She was not sure if what she was seeing was in the ball or in her mind but she knew that it didn't matter. The vision ended and Mary sat back and considered what she had learned. She had never thought of herself as a leader before.

## SCRYING

It is great if you happen to get a prophetic dream or if you meet an oracle or a prophet who can help you out with your problems, but suppose you just want some simple answers without traveling to a distant temple and spending lots of money? The first chapter discussed directing dreams through incubation, and the second chapter mentioned automatic writing, but there is another means of divination that can provide answers in a simple way while the questioner is awake and in control. This type of divination is called **scrying**.

**Figure 3.1** *Mary's crystal ball.* (Robert M. Place)

Unlike many other divination terms, scrying is not Greek in origin. It is a shortened form of the Old English word *descry*, which means to reveal or make out. Scrying is a means of obtaining a vision by looking into a transparent or shiny surface. The most common tool associated with scrying today is a crystal or glass ball, but those objects can be expensive and unnecessary. People have used all sorts of tools for scrying throughout history, from pools of water to shiny fingernails. Have you ever sat looking at a lake and letting your thoughts drift? That may be how scrying got started. It most likely began with prehistoric peoples looking at the surface of a pool of water. This type of scrying can also be called **hydromancy**, from the Greek word for water, *hydro*, plus *mancy* (*Manteia*, divination).

Historical accounts report Native American tribes used pools in this way to get a vision about the best place to hunt or to find lost objects. As with other forms of divination, certain people seem to be gifted at scrying and other people will seek them out. In tribal cultures they are referred to as shamans or priests, and in European culture they are called magicians. There are accounts of Polynesian priests on islands in the Pacific Ocean who, when looking for a thief, would dig a hole in the doorway of the burglarized house, fill it with water, and see the thief in the water. They believed the doorway would retain the memory of the thief passing through, and the water would reflect the memory.[10] The Wicked Witch of the West in the movie, *The Wizard of Oz*, had a magic cauldron filled with a liquid (she did not like water much) that she would look into to see what Dorothy was doing no matter where the girl was. She was scrying. The ancient Babylonians were said to have sacred stone bowls filled with liquid that their priests used in the same way. More recently, the Zulus of South Africa had similar vessels, as did shamans in Siberia. The Egyptians, on the other hand, just poured some black ink into the palm of their hands when they wanted a magic scrying pool.

Many folk traditions instruct scryers to practice at night and capture the reflection of the moon on the surface of the water to make the viewing-water more special. Prehistoric peoples probably had sacred places that were used for water-viewing because they were more inspiring than any old mud puddle. Historic examples of this include the Temple of Ceres at Patras or Patrae, on the gulf of Patras in Greece, which had a magic fountain in front. A sick person could tie a mirror to a cord and lower it down into the fountain until it touched the surface of the water. Then he or she could look into the mirror in the

## Nostradamus

Perhaps the most famous scryer in history is the French Renaissance seer M. Michel Nostradamus (1503-1566). There is some disagreement, however, as to whether or not he actually scryed. In 1550 Nostradamus began publishing a yearly almanac. In Nostradamus's time the main purpose of almanacs was to make predictions of the weather and other events that were derived from astrology. Nostradamus was very successful at selling his almanacs and it seemed that some of his predictions came true. He was even summoned by the queen, Catherine de Medici, to make astrology charts for the royal family. Inspired by his success he took on the ambitious task of creating books of predictions for the future of the world, from his lifetime until the end of the world. The result was *The Prophecies*, which were collections of predictions in the form of four line poems, called quatrains. Nostradamus published it in three volumes, which came out in 1555, 1557, and 1558.

Although they are filled with predictions of horrible things like plagues, floods, earthquakes, wars, and murders, *The Prophecies* are

**Figure 3.2** *French engraving of Michel Nostradamus.* (Stefano Bianchetti/Corbis)

water and see their chances for recovery. It would have been better to look for a cure but that is the way the practice has been reported by ancient writers.[11]

Nostradamus's most popular work. Since 1555 they have rarely been out of print and there have been over 200 editions published. To make his predictions Nostradamus made use of astrology and Bible interpretation, but he also described going into a meditative trance state to bring everything together and see clearly into the future. In his descriptions Nostradamus mentions a "bronze tripod," which he compares to the three-legged stool that the oracle of Delphi sat on.[15] Historians are not sure if he was comparing himself to the oracle or if he had an object with three legs that helped him to meditate. In spite of this uncertainty, many writers over the centuries have claimed that Nostradamus focused on a bowl of water supported on a bronze tripod when he peered into the future. Although these writers have made Nostradamus one of the most famous scryers in the world, it is uncertain if he actually was a scryer.

Nostradamus has been credited by various authors with predicting the great fire in London in 1666, the rise of Napoleon, the rise and demise of Hitler, the September 11, 2001, terrorist attack on New York's World Trade Center, and many other disasters. None of his predictions are dated, however, and they are written in a vague symbolic style that allows them to be applied to many situations. It is a matter of opinion as to whether or not he has been successful in his predictions and most scholars and scientists are not impressed. In all of these examples people have credited him with a prediction only after the event has happened. If predictions are to be useful they should warn about a harmful event beforehand so that people can avoid it. In fact, it seems that is what Nostradamus was hoping to accomplish, to change history for the better.[16] He would probably be disappointed with the credit he is getting for predicting disasters that no one was able to avoid.

This story brings us to the next tool that is popular for scrying: the mirror. A mirror resembles the surface of a smooth pond, frozen so that it can be conveniently carried around. In the fairy tale

*Snow White*, the wicked queen looked into her magic mirror to see who was the fairest. She was scrying. In *The Canterbury Tales*, written by Geoffrey Chaucer (1343-1400), travelers amuse each other with stories while on a trip. In one story, a squire tells of a magic mirror that can be used to see anywhere in the kingdom, sort of like the witch's cauldron in the story of Oz. In *The Faerie Queene*, an Arthurian legend written by Edmund Spenser (1552-1599), the wizard Merlin uses his magic to create a magic mirror with the same power. It seems that these magic mirrors are often associated with magicians, but the occult author Emile Grillot de Givry (1874-1929) tells us that the queen of France, Catherine de Medici (1519-1589), had a mirror in which she could see everything that was happening in France. Also, the French king Henri IV (1553-1610) had access to a similar mirror.[12]

Glass mirrors were not used in Europe until the thirteenth century. In the ancient world mirrors were not made of glass but of a plate of polished metal, like bronze or silver. Glass mirrors are coated with silver. The ancient Greeks mostly had magic bronze mirrors, so did the Indians, and the Chinese. It is not surprising, therefore, that some heroes in legends also use the polished blade of a sword or a shield for scrying. One of the most unusual tools, yet one of the most readily available, is a polished thumbnail. This is a popular scrying tool in Arab countries where the best scryers are young boys, who tend to lose the gift by age 10 or 11.[13] Often, Renaissance magicians used mirrors that were glass with the back painted black instead of silvered. Perhaps they were trying to imitate another ancient scrying tool, a piece of polished black stone called onyx. But, the most popular stones for scrying were transparent.

It seems that the first people known to use stones for scrying were the Celts (pronounced *kelts*), an ancient people of the British Isles. The Celtic priests were called druids, and Roman historians said that the druids used stones such as beryl or polished quartz for scrying. Discoveries that archeologists have made confirm that the druids or their predecessors were probably scrying with polished stones as early as 2000 BCE. In the Middle Ages the practice continued among the Scottish people. By the time of the Renaissance, John Dee (1527-1608), an astrologer, scientist, magician, and a real-life Merlin to Queen Elizabeth I (1533-1603), was using a polished quartz crystal egg for scrying. These eggs seemed to be popular in England.[14] In other parts of Europe the quartz crystal ball developed in the Middle Ages and the Renaissance. Many other people around the world have used different magical stones of various shapes for divination but the crystal ball, which became the favorite tool of Gypsies and carnival psychics, has become the standard object associated with scrying today.

# 4

# Omens

In the spring of 289 BCE, Quintus got out of bed early. He washed in the bath in the center of his house and then wrapped himself in his expensive, white, wool toga. He was one of the nine Roman priests called *augurs*, who were honored to be the spokesmen for Jupiter, the king of the gods. Jupiter lived in the heavens and to communicate with him Quintus would have to go to a special field, called the Auguraculum, on Capitoline Hill, in the heart of Rome. When he got there he would look into the sky for Jupiter's messengers, the birds, and interpret their actions to determine Jupiter's opinion on the matter at hand.

The matter at hand this time was a planned commercial sea voyage. Many Romans would not think of agreeing to any major decision about politics, war, commerce, or even marriage without first getting Jupiter's opinion, which could be favorable or unfavorable. As one of the official diviners of the Roman Republic, Quintus was not involved in obtaining predictions from the god but only in asking the question, "Do I have Jupiter's favor to do what I intend to do?" Jupiter's opinion might effect the outcome and certainly with Jupiter's blessing an action was more likely to succeed, but Romans were more concerned with not offending the king of the gods. Asking Jupiter for his blessing was sort of like asking for your father's permission before borrowing the family car.

**Figure 4.1** *Roman augurs divine the opinions of the gods by observing the behavior of hens.* (Mary Evans Picture Library/The Image Works)

The augurs were highly respected and it was a great honor to be chosen as one. Quintus was one of the four augurs chosen from the upper class, called patricians. The Romans also chose five augurs from the lower class, called plebeians. All of the augurs had to be trained to learn the meanings of the various types of wild birds, the sound that they made, their flight patterns, eating habits, and most of all, whether they approached the Auguraculum from the left, which is called *sinister* in Latin, or from the right, which is called *dexter* in Latin. The name sinister might suggest that if the birds flew in from the left it was a bad sign but it depended on the type of birds. It was bad if ravens came from the left, but if crows did it was good.[17] There was a lot to learn but the augurs had time because they were chosen to serve for life.

Quintus arrived early and climbed the hill to enter the Auguraculum. He walked up onto the small mound in the center of the field and lit the incense in the bronze burner as he prayed to Jupiter for a sign.

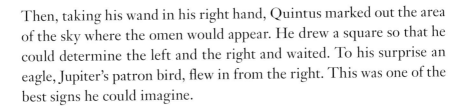

Then, taking his wand in his right hand, Quintus marked out the area of the sky where the omen would appear. He drew a square so that he could determine the left and the right and waited. To his surprise an eagle, Jupiter's patron bird, flew in from the right. This was one of the best signs he could imagine.

## OMENS IN THE SKY

Most ancient people believed that the spirits, the gods, or God wanted to talk to them. This communication happened through dreams and in waking life through signs sent by the divine. These signs could be any natural object or event that was meaningful to the viewer. These were omens. Basically, omens are a way of treating events as if they are dreams and the things and actions are symbols.

At its worst this can turn into a superstitious belief in which a certain thing is always a symbol of good or bad luck, such as the superstitions that breaking a mirror or stepping on a crack is bad luck and finding a coin on the ground or a four-leafed clover is good luck. Similar beliefs exist around the world, but in different cultures some of the same symbols can be bad in one and good in another. For example, in England a black cat crossing your path is good luck, while in the United States it is bad luck.[18] Yet if we treat events and objects in our life like the unique symbols in our dreams that are meaningful for us in a personal way, there is no difference between omens and Jung's synchronicity, which was discussed in the Introduction. Then omens can be powerful messages from our Higher Self, like the kingfisher that Jung found by the lake. In ancient cultures there is often a mixture of both types of omens, some that seem silly and some that have marked profound changes in the lives of individuals or in the beliefs of entire cultures.

All ancient civilizations had gifted people trained to look for signs or omens from the gods. The ancient Sumerians and Babylonians, like many people, primarily looked to the sky, the home of the gods, for omens. This practice eventually led to the development of astrology. Because Jupiter was the god of the heavens, the augurs of ancient Rome looked to the flight of birds for omens but they also practiced **brontoscopy**, the interpretation of lightning or thunder as a message from Jupiter. Likewise, in ancient Greece lightning was considered a sign from Zeus, the king of the gods; in India it was a sign from Indra, the god of weather and war; in Eastern Europe among the Slavs it was a sign from Perun, the king of the gods; and in the Germanic countries it was a sign from Thor, the god of thunder and strength. Even in the Bible, lightning and thunder are signs of Jehovah's presence. They mark the sacrifice of Christ on the cross, and foretell the second coming.

Christ's birth was marked by a different heavenly omen, an unusually bright star called the Star of Bethlehem. Changes in the night sky were always looked upon as omens but not necessarily favorable ones. The word *disaster*, for example, is derived from the Latin word for star, *astro*. Originally it may have referred to an unfavorable star in an astrology chart but it could also refer to the disruption a comet makes in the night sky. Many early cultures considered a comet an attacker in the sky and, therefore, a bad omen. Comets as bad omens are mentioned in the story of Gilgamesh, in Revelation in the Bible, and in Nostradamus's predictions. Sometimes, however, a comet may be interpreted as a good omen.

People have also always found eclipses of the sun or moon to be impressive signs from the gods but often the eclipse of the moon is more impressive because people can actually watch it. The Babylonians thought of a lunar eclipse as a sign of the moon's anger, and that was bad. In China, traditionally an eclipse of the moon is thought of as a dragon eating the moon, another bad omen. To scare away the dragon, people would come out of their houses and make noise by banging pots and other things.

Some of the most important events in history have been marked by signs in the sky. In 312 CE the Roman emperor Constantine

(r. 306-337) had to fight an important battle at Milvian Bridge, outside of Rome. Before the battle he saw an omen in the shape of a cross above the sun in the sky and realized it was an omen from Christ that assured his victory. Because of this omen Constantine became the first Christian emperor and helped make Christianity the religion of Rome.

According to legend, in 832, before an important battle with the English, the Scottish king Angus Mac Fergus (r. 820-834) saw in the sky an omen in the form of a white X, which was the shape of the cross on which Scotland's patron, St. Andrew, was martyred. He won the battle and, to commemorate the omen, the Scottish flag today has a white X on a blue field.[19]

## EARTHLY OMENS

Not all omens are so huge and celestial. Beside the augurs in ancient Rome, there were official diviners, called **haruspices**, who looked for omens in the livers of animals sacrificed to the gods. Similarly Scottish diviners looked at an animal's shoulder blade for omens, and the Chinese were said to look at tortoise shells. The equivalent of haruspices can be found in most ancient cultures. The animals that received the honor of being sacrificed would probably have liked it better if people continued to look to the sky for omens, but not all earthly omens are so bloody.

People have also looked for omens in ordinary household objects. One of the most common objects is a book. This is called **bibliomancy**. *Biblio* is derived from the Greek for book. To practice bibliomancy, all you have to do is ask a question of your Higher Self, open a book to a random page, point to any sentence or paragraph on that page, and read your answer. This works especially well with a book that you feel is important or sacred. Ancient Greeks used the *Iliad* and the *Odyssey*, Hindus used the Vedas, Islamic people used the Koran, and Christians have used the Bible for this for centuries.

Almost any object can be used as a source of omens in this way. For example people have looked for omens in the patterns or shapes of tea leaves left in the bottom of their cup. This is called **tasseomancy**. *Tasse* is derived from the French word for cup. This term also applies if we look for omens in what is left in the bottom of our coffee cup. In the Middle East, people tend to look at the residue in an emptied wine glass instead. Similarly, looking for omens in the movements of a candle flame is called **lychnomancy**; looking for omens in the movements of horses, like the ancient Celts did, is called **hippomancy**; and looking at the behavior of cats is called **ailuromancy**. The list seems endless and to name the method just find the Greek word for the thing you are looking at and add *mancy*. You can make up your own.

## OMENS IN THE BODY

One of the most common places that humans have sought omens is the human body. For example, people have read the lines on foreheads, which is called **metoposcopy**. This practice was developed by sixteenth century physician and astrologer, Jerome Cardan (1501-1576). Basically, he assigned the lines on the forehead to different planets and read them like a **horoscope**. Another method is to read bumps on top of a person's head, or look at the shape of his or her skull to determine a person's character. This is called **phrenology** and was developed by a German physician, Franz Joseph Gall (1758-1828), in the nineteenth century. An older method of discerning character is to look at the shape of the face. This is called **physiognomy** and it can be traced back to ancient Greece. The most popular and perhaps the most ancient place to look for omens on the body, however, is the hand.

Reading the hand, more commonly known as palm reading or **palmistry**, is also called **chiromancy**. Palmistry is one of the oldest forms of divination. Palm prints found in cave paintings in France show us that prehistoric people up to 30,000 years ago were fascinated by the palm and believed that it had magical power. There is evidence that the ancient Babylonians, Egyptians, Greeks, Hebrews, and Chinese saw a connection between the features of the hand and a person's fate. Ancient India, however, seems to be the source of modern methods of palmistry and it is possible that the Chinese,

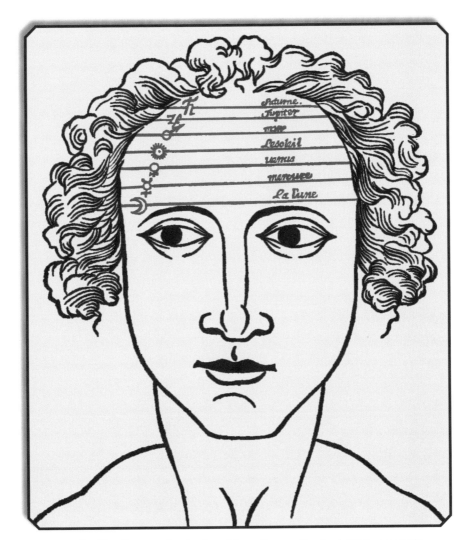

**Figure 4.2**   *The lines on the forehead from Jerome Cardan's* Metoposcopia, *Paris 1658.*

---

## Fatalistic Predictions

Jerome Cardan, who invented metoposcopy, was also a devoted astrologer. Unfortunately, however, he seems to have taken a fatalistic approach and aimed at prediction rather than true divination. According to legend, Cardan used astrology to predict that he would die when he reached the age of 75. To assure the accuracy of his prediction he is said to have starved himself to death when he reached that age.[20]

---

the Tibetans, and the Greeks all learned the art from the Indians. Palmistry is also associated with Gypsies, who originated in India, and, at one time, it was thought that they brought the art to Western Europe. There is evidence, though, that palmistry was already taught in the West in the Middle Ages and Gypsies arrived later in the fifteenth century.

Here is a brief outline of how palmistry is done. The first thing a palmist looks at is the shape of the hand, to see if it is square or long and if the fingers are longer than the palm or the other way around. Next the palmist determines the proportions and the shape of the fingertips. There are four finger shapes that relate to four temperaments:

1  **square**: careful
2  **pointed**: sensitive
3  **conic**: flexible
4  **spatulate**: dynamic

Then there are the lines in the palm to consider (See Figure 4.3). Besides the minor lines, there are four principal lines:

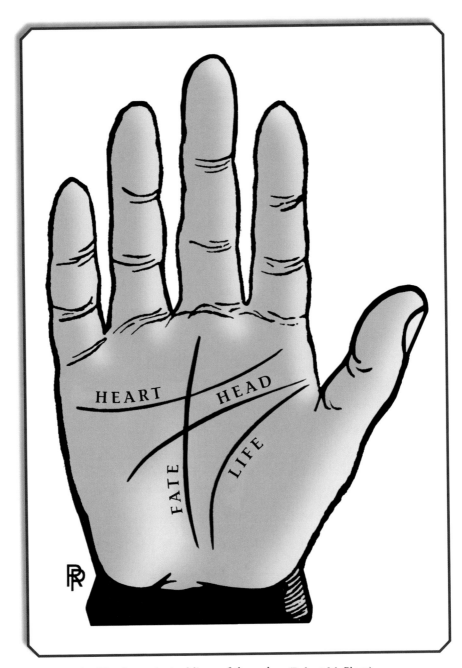

**Figure 4.3**  *The four principal lines of the palm.*  (Robert M. Place)

1 **heart line**: tells of your emotional life

2 **head line**: tells of the quality your thinking

3 **life line**: shows your vitality and health (no, the length of your life line does not determine the length of your life)

4 **fate line**: shows if you are settled or unsettled

Generally, deep and straight lines tend to be positive and splintered, wavy, or shallow lines less positive. In addition, there are the mounds on the palm, with eight principal mounds, each associated with one of the seven planets of the ancients, except there are two for Mars, an upper and a lower (see Figure 4.4 for positions).

1 **Venus**: health and sexuality

2 **Moon**: sensitivity and imagination

3 **Mars**: courage and temper (split into an upper and lower mound)

4 **Jupiter**: selfishness or generosity

5 **Saturn**: ambition

6 **Apollo or Sun**: taste and self-image

7 **Mercury**: thinking and wit

The larger mounds show overdeveloped traits and flat mounds are underdeveloped traits. Medium size mounds are best. The palmist also needs to consider all those funny little marks like Xs and Os and how they interact with everything else. You can see the five principle minor marks in Table 4.1.

Although different palmist may have different ideas about what these things in the hand mean, traditionally, a palmist would look at each part of the hand in this way and tell a person all about their character and their life in the past and in the future. At their worst, palmists have actually tried to tell clients when they will marry, how many children they will have, when they will get sick, and how long they

| TABLE 4.1: **The Minor Marks of the Hand** | | |
|:---:|:---:|:---:|
| | **FORK** | choice |
| | **ISLAND** | weakness |
| | **GRILLE** | obstacle |
| | **CROSS** | negative influence |
| | **STAR** | positive influence |

will live. This is not good. Any reputable palmist will tell you that the lines in your hand will change as you grow and make changes in your life. Therefore, your future will look different as your hand changes. This is noticeable in the differences between the left and right hands. The hand used the least will show traits present since childhood while the dominant hand, the one used most, will show the changes since then. A palm reading, therefore, is really about the present and a good palmist will help a client understand his or her strengths and weakness and help point out where work is needed to improve one's life.

Modern palmists realize it is helpful to discuss the separate parts of the hand, but they maintain that the art depends on putting it all together and looking at the hand as a whole. For example, when someone smiles it is not something that just happens with the mouth; the whole face is involved. Good palmists will look at the hand like a face and see if it is smiling or frowning.

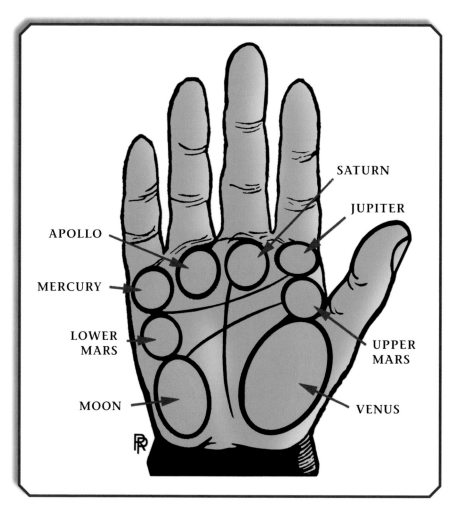

**Figure 4.4** *The principal mounds of the palm.* (Robert M. Place)

# NUMBERS AS OMENS

Have you ever wondered what your lucky number is? In the modern world numbers are one of the most popular places to look for omens. This is called numerology.

Numbers are everywhere, but the most popular place to look for significant numbers is one's birth date or name. Birth dates already exist in numbers, if a number is substituted for the month instead of the word, but to use a name, the letters must be converted into numbers. In ancient Greek and Hebrew this was easy because people commonly used the letters of the alphabet for writing numbers. In the modern world, however, a number must be assigned to each letter. The most common way is to simply assign the numbers one through 26 to the 26 letters of the alphabet and then add up all of the numbers for each letter in the name. But, to find meaning in the number, it must be reduced to one of the first 10 numbers. This is accomplished by adding all of the numbers together until you have one of the first 10.

For example, the letters in Robert are assigned R-18, O-15, B-2, E-5, R-18, and T-20. These numbers add up to 78 (18+15+2+5+18+20=78). Now to get a simpler number, add the 7 and 8 together to get 15. Then add the 1 and 5 to get 6. The numerical omen for Robert is six.

Okay, but what does six mean? There is disagreement as to what each number signifies, but most Western numerologists (there is also a Chinese system) trace this form of divination back to the famous Greek philosopher and mathematician Pythagoras (582-507 BCE) and try to base their interpretations on his teachings about the quality of numbers. Pythagoras is said to have studied with the Babylonians and Egyptians. His numerical symbolism was adopted by most Western mystics, such as alchemists (people who, while trying to make lead into gold, developed chemistry), and kabbalists (Jewish mystics and magicians). Here is a list of common meanings for the first 10 numbers that are related to Pythagorean ideas.

- **One**: The primary symbol of unity, one is independent, creative, original, ambitious, determined, and self-assured.
- **Two**: The number of duality, two symbolizes both harmony and opposition, a peacemaker and one who gives an argument.
- **Three**: The creative result to the interaction of one and two, three is a creative solution, an expression of personality, sociable, friendly, outgoing, kind, positive, and optimistic.
- **Four**: The completion of the physical world with its four directions, seasons, and elements, four is a worker, practical, trustworthy, helpful, steady, logical, and self-disciplined.
- **Five**: The number of the spiritual essence beyond the physical four, five is a an agent for change, adaptable, intelligent, freedom-loving, romantic, resourceful, witty, curious, flexible, and accommodating.
- **Six**: The result of two threes added together, six is the number of relationships, harmony, love, peace, and beauty.
- **Seven**: Everybody's favorite lucky number and the number of known planets in the ancient world, seven is mystical, introspective, intuitive, psychic, wise, and reserved.
- **Eight**: A doubling of four turning a square, with four points, into a cube, with eight; eight is ambitious, business-minded, practical, leading, authoritative, successful, courageous, accomplished, organized, and materialistic.
- **Nine**: The last of the single digit numbers and the number associated with heaven by ancient mystics, nine is humanitarian, sympathetic, helpful, emotional, tolerant, active, and determined.
- **Ten**: The return to unity after the completion of the series, 10 is a number of completion, perfection, and achievement.

To these 10, modern numerologists have added zero, which symbolizes the unconscious and untapped potential, the power number 11, a humanitarian innovator, and the power number 22, the visionary master builder who is idealistic and yet practical.

# Astrology

It was 44 BCE and Octavian's adopted father Julius Caesar (100-44 BCE) had made himself the sole ruler of Rome, and then on March 15, the ill-fated Ides of March, he was assassinated on the floor of the senate, stabbed 32 times by a group of senators. Octavian knew that as Caesar's heir he would have to avenge his father's death, and there would be a war between him and Brutus, Cassius, and the other assassins. This war would decide the fate of Rome, but it would also decide his fate. Understandably, Octavian was worried about his future.

Octavian's friend Agrippa took him to see Theogenes, one of the most famous astrologers in Rome. Early in the afternoon Octavian and Agrippa visited the astrologer in his open-air office on the roof of one of Rome's tall buildings. Agrippa went first. He provided Theogenes with the exact time and date of his birth,

**Figure 5.1** *Augustus, the first Roman emperor.* (Araldo de Luca/ Corbis)

**Figure 5.2** *The Capricorn coin of Augustus.*

and Theogenes began drawing up an astrological chart with symbols depicting the position of the seven planets known at that time in relation to the constellations or signs of the zodiac on that date. Then Theogenes began to interpret the chart. He had such grand things to say about Agrippa's personality and fate that when it was time for Octavian to tell the astrologer his birth information he refused for fear that his chart could not compare to Agrippa's.

Luckily, Agrippa was able to bolster his friend's courage and Octavian did tell Theogenes what he needed to know to make the chart. Octavian sat patiently while Theogenes worked, but once the chart was complete, to his surprise the astrologer knelt before him and kissed his hand.

"You have the chart of a great ruler," Theogenes said. "You will be one of greatest rulers that Rome has ever known. Your sun is in Libra, which is the sign that rules Rome, but more importantly the sign coming over the horizon at the moment of your birth, called the rising sign, is Capricorn, which is ruled by the planet Saturn, the god who presided over the golden-age when he was on Earth. You will bring a new golden-age to Rome."

Octavian was overjoyed. He wanted to let everyone know about such an impressive chart, so he had a copy carved into a slab of marble and set in the center of the city for everyone to read. Years later, after he was victorious at the pivotal battles of Philippi and Actium, he became the emperor of Rome and changed his name to Caesar Augustus (63 BCE-14 CE). He ruled for 41 years and started an area of peace and prosperity that lasted 200 years, called the *Pax Romana*. To remind people that it was his destiny to be a great emperor he had a silver coin struck that depicted his rising sign Capricorn, the sea-goat, holding the world (see Figure 5.2).[21]

## FROM OMENS TO STAR CHARTS

The ancient Sumerians and Babylonians of Mesopotamia, like people for thousands of years before them, looked to the sky for omens from their gods, particularly in the night sky. Viewed from Earth the stars in the night sky keep their positions the same in relation to each other, which is why people can always see the recognizable star patterns, called constellations. People have named these the constellations after people, animals, and things from mythology, like Hercules or Pegasus the winged horse. All of the constellations move together as a unit through the night sky, rising in the east and setting in the west.

Against this pattern of lights there are other, brighter objects that move at a different pace. Some of these wanderers even occasionally move west to east against the current. These objects were called planets, which is based on the Greek word for wanderer, *planetes.* Although the planets seem to wander, they do stay on a path in the sky. This path is called the **ecliptic** by astronomers, and the circle of 12 constellations that this path cuts through is called the **zodiac**, a term derived from the Greek word *zoidiakos*, meaning a circle of animal figures. Without a telescope only seven heavenly objects considered planets by the ancients are visible from Earth. They are the Sun, the Moon, Mercury, Venus, Mars, Jupiter, and Saturn.

Astronomers like Nicolaus Copernicus (1473-1543) later determined that the sun and the moon are not planets, but are a star and a satellite, respectively, and that there are actually eight planets not seven. Ancient people could not see Uranus or Neptune because they did not have telescopes. Until people like Copernicus made more accurate observations of the solar system, most people assumed that the stars and planets moved around Earth. Ancient astronomers figured that Earth was standing still in the center with the planets and the stars rotating around it. To them, therefore, the sun and moon were wanderers like the other planets and Earth was not a planet because it was standing still. Also, those seven unassailable bright wandering bodies seemed really important. To ancient people they seemed like the rulers of the skies. By the time the earliest cultures were writing about these things, these wanderers were considered gods.

From 1795 to 1750 BCE, Mesopotamia was united under the rule of the Babylonian king Hammurabi (1810-1750 BCE). Although people were tracking the movement of the planets and looking to them for predictions before this, it was during this period that the first astrological texts were written. At first astrology was just concerned with the welfare of the king and the kingdom, but by 600 BCE astrologers began to make charts for individuals. To accomplish this, astrologers standardized the 12 constellations of the zodiac, now called signs, by assigning each 30 degrees on the giant circle of the ecliptic so that the 12 signs filled all 360 degrees of the circle. Then charts could be drawn to show exactly where each planetary god was at the moment of a person's birth. Individual charts could be used to show a person's character and predict the challenges that he or she would face in life. This is called a natal chart or a horoscope. From Mesopotamia astrology spread to India and Egypt and later spread north to Persia and west to the Greek and Roman world.

The ancient Greeks made some significant contributions to astrology. Although some Greek philosophers wondered if Earth actually circled around the sun, most Greeks still believed that Earth was in the center of the universe. In their theory, Earth was a sphere floating motionless in the center of the universe with the seven planets circling it. Each planet was thought to be connected to a giant, hollow, crystal ball that rotated around Earth, with each planet's ball nested inside the next and the Earth in the center. The arrangement was similar to Russian nesting dolls, where each one opens like a box to reveal another, smaller one inside, then another, and so on. Encasing the outermost crystal was the eighth sphere of the constellations and beyond that was the home of the gods. The Greeks believed that the soul of each person emerged from this heavenly home at birth. The new soul began its descent into the physical world by departing heaven through one of the constellations in the zodiac, like a doorway, and then the soul used the planets as a ladder or stairway to Earth. At each rung or step, the god of that planet clothed the soul in qualities that would become its body and its personality on Earth. This is the origin of the traditional lists of seven virtues and seven vices. The astrological natal chart was designed to map this journey.

In the second century the astronomer and mathematician Claudius Ptolemy (90-168 CE), who lived in Alexandria, Egypt, which at that time was part of the Greek or Hellenized world, created a neat model of this cosmos. He also wrote four texts, called the *Tetrabiblios*, which are the basis of modern astrology. In Greek *tetra* means four, and this title means four books. Ptolemy measured the speed at which

**Figure 5.3** *Ptolemy's ladder of the planets from the fastest to the slowest, with the time it takes each planet to complete one trip through the zodiac.* (Robert M. Place)

each planet seemed to move through the ecliptic and organized them with the fastest closest to Earth and the slowest closest to the sphere of the zodiac (See Figure 5.3). Ptolemy's model was the standard used in education throughout the Middle Ages and the Renaissance until it was replaced by Copernicus's model, which was introduced in 1543 but did not reach full acceptance until the seventeenth century. Although astrologers no longer believe in this theory of the universe and have added the influence of Uranus, Neptune, and Pluto (which until recently was considered a planet) to their charts, modern astrological charts are not that different than the ancient Greek ones.

## THE PARTS OF A HOROSCOPE

In the past, to draw up a horoscope or natal chart required some skill at mathematics and an **ephemeris**, which is a book listing the positions of the planets for each day of the year for each year covered. Today computer programs are available to provide this information. Astrologers may plug in the hour, day, month, year, and place of a client's birth and the computer produces a horoscope without mistakes in the math. But the astrologer still has to interpret the chart. Interpreting a chart requires much more information than can be

**Figure 5.4** *Horoscope by Erhard S. Schon, Nurnberg 1515.*

discussed here, but good books on astrology that cover the topic in-depth are available. What this book will do is help you to understand what you are looking at and explain each part of the chart.

A horoscope chart looks like a circle with a smaller circle inside forming a ring like a doughnut that has been cut into 12 equal parts. These 12 slices are the **houses**, which will be explained later. On this diagram an astrologer or a computer program will write symbols for the 12 houses of the zodiac and the 10 planets (once Uranus, Neptune, and Pluto have been added to the seven ancient ones), showing their positions at the moment of their client's birth. Then connecting lines are drawn describing the relationships among the planets, which are noted with other symbols.

Figure 5.4 is an elaborate horoscope drawn by German artist Er-hard S. Schon in 1515. Because Schon placed the planets, the signs, and the houses each in their own circle and fully illustrated each subject instead of just using symbols, he has provided a good tool for discussing the parts of the chart. Notice that the innermost circle has a picture of a landscape on Earth. The inner circle of all charts represents Earth and the outer circles represent the sky. Beyond the circles, Schon has depicted the four winds and God in heaven. In the second ring outside of Earth Schon has depicted the ancient gods who ruled the planets, and over the shoulder of each he has drawn the symbol that astrologers use for each planet. Because this was drawn in 1515 there are only the ancient seven. The figure near the top with the sword and the circle with an arrow coming out of it is Mars. Continuing clockwise the planets are Saturn, Jupiter, Mercury, the Moon, Venus, and the Sun. To this list modern astrologers add Uranus, Neptune, and Pluto. Each planet represents certain qualities, which are derived from the ancient gods after whom they are named. You can see the symbols for each planet and a list of some of its qualities in Table 5.1.

Each planet is interpreted in the horoscope by how it interacts with the sign that it inhabits. The 12 signs can be seen in the next

TABLE 5.1: **The Planets**

| | | |
|---|---|---|
| ☉ | **SUN** | most important planet because it represents the ego or consciousness |
| ☽ | **MOON** | second most important because it represents the unconscious, the inner person |
| ☿ | **MERCURY** | represents the realm of the mind, self-knowledge, communication, and travel |
| ♀ | **VENUS** | love, marriage, luxury, and beauty, the ideal female |
| ♂ | **MARS** | action, energy, assertion, and aggression, the ideal male |
| ♃ | **JUPITER** | growth, expansion, abundance, religion, and higher education |
| ♄ | **SATURN** | limitation, restriction, challenges, difficulties, discipline, and the shadow |
| ♅ | **URANUS** | unpredictable, revolutionary, antiauthoritarian, visionary, and progressive |
| ♆ | **NEPTUNE** | intangible and idealistic, the planet of mysticism but also delusion |
| ♇ | **PLUTO** | this planet was only discovered in 1930 and its influence is mysterious and not yet fully understood; recently astronomers demoted it to a non-planet |

largest circle. Starting with the goat with a fish tail at the top, which is Capricorn, and continuing clockwise, they are: Sagittarius the archer, Scorpio the scorpion, Libra the scales, Virgo the virgin, Leo the lion, Cancer the crab, Gemini the twins, Taurus the bull, Aries the ram, Pisces the two fish, and Aquarius the figure pouring water. Each of the signs has one of three qualities:

1  **Cardinal,** which means it marks the change of one of the four seasons

2  **Fixed,** which means it is solidly in the middle of a season

3  **Mutable,** which means that it is starting to change seasons.

The signs are also each assigned one of the four ancient **elements**—earth, air, fire, or water—which relate to four **aspects** of personality as seen in this chart.

1  **Earth**: material concerns

2  **Air**: thinking

3  **Fire**: creative energy

4  **Water**: emotions

Besides this, each sign has certain planets that are more at home there. To learn more about the signs and to learn which planet is at home in each look at Table 5.2. The date under each name tells when the sun is in that sign. The sun is considered the most important planet for gathering information about one's personality. Another important aspect is the **rising sign**, which is the sign that is coming over the horizon in the east at the moment of someone's birth. Astrologers also pay attention to the sign on the opposite side descending in the west, called the **descendent**; to the sign at the top of the sky, called the **midheaven**; and again to the opposite sign called the **nadir**. Together these are called the four angles.

The last and largest ring on Schon's chart is the ring of the houses. Because the 12 signs keep moving through the sky, astrologers wanted

*(text continues on page 74)*

TABLE 5.2: **Signs of the Zodiac**  *(Illustrations by Robert M. Place)*

| | | |
|---|---|---|
| | **Aries**<br>March 21–April 20<br>Cardinal<br>Fire<br>the house of Mars | positive<br>straightforward<br>energetic<br>determined<br>temperamental<br>crude<br>impatient |
| | **Taurus**<br>April 21–May 21<br>Fixed<br>Earth<br>the house of Venus | down-to-earth<br>calm<br>conservative<br>practical<br>sensual<br>stubborn<br>materialistic |
| | **Gemini**<br>May 22–June21<br>Mutable<br>Air<br>the house of Mercury | jovial<br>imaginative<br>talkative<br>persuasive<br>versatile<br>irresponsible<br>superficial |
| | **Cancer**<br>June 22–July 22<br>Cardinal<br>Water<br>the house of the Moon | emotional<br>protective<br>home-loving<br>shrewd<br>loyal<br>shy<br>lives in a shell |

*(continues)*

TABLE 5.2: **Signs of the Zodiac** *(continued)*

| | | |
|---|---|---|
| ♌ | **Leo**<br>July 23–August 23<br>Fixed<br>Fire<br>the house of the Sun | bossy<br>independent<br>idealistic<br>warm<br>center of attention<br>egotistic<br>extravagant |
| ♍ | **Virgo**<br>August 24–<br>September 23<br>Mutable<br>Earth<br>the house of Mercury | precise<br>economic<br>industrious<br>modest<br>analytical<br>critical<br>sense of inferiority |
| ♎ | **Libra**<br>September 24–<br>October 23<br>Cardinal<br>Air<br>the house of Venus | diplomatic<br>positive<br>seeks balance &<br>reconciliation<br>considerate<br>artistic<br>indecisive<br>procrastinator |
| ♏ | **Scorpio**<br>October 24–<br>November 22<br>Fixed<br>Water<br>the house of<br>Mars & Pluto | steadfast<br>secretive<br>intense<br>intuitive<br>intimate<br>cynical<br>easy to anger |

TABLE 5.2: **Signs of the Zodiac**

| | | |
|---|---|---|
| | **Sagittarius**<br>November 23–<br>December 21<br>Mutable<br>Fire<br>the house of Jupiter | versatile<br>fun loving<br>optimistic<br>traveler<br>liberal<br>irresponsible<br>restless |
| | **Capricorn**<br>December 22–<br>January 20<br>Cardinal<br>Earth<br>the house of Saturn | economical<br>ambitious<br>cautious<br>systematic<br>productive<br>self-conscious<br>snobbish |
| | **Aquarius**<br>January 21–<br>February 19<br>Fixed<br>Air<br>the house of Saturn<br>and Uranus | sociable<br>observant<br>independent<br>eccentric<br>sensible<br>arrogant<br>stubborn |
| | **Pisces**<br>February 20–<br>March 20<br>Mutable<br>Water<br>the house of<br>Jupiter & Neptune | unpredictable<br>imaginative<br>inner directed<br>creative<br>spiritual<br>absent-minded<br>dreamer<br>escapist |

a way to measure this movement. So, they visualized the circle of the sky as divided into 12 houses each taking up 30 degrees, like the signs, but standing still. Each house has a sign that is more at home there, but the signs move to different houses and the house that the sign is in at the moment of birth tells more about it in a person's chart. They are numbered counterclockwise from one to 12, with one at the left side of the circle. Here is a list of the houses with their meanings and how they relate to Schon's illustrations.

- **1st House**: This is the house of the body and of the self-image; the woman in the illustration is giving birth to a new body.
- **2nd House**: This is the house of money and possessions.
- **3rd House**: This is the house of environment, family ties, and early education.
- **4th House**: This house speaks about home life; it might be called the house of the house.
- **5th House**: This is the house of creativity and love, including children, creative projects, business, and art.
- **6th House**: This is the house of service and health.
- **7th House**: This is the house of marriage and partnership; the illustration shows a wedding.
- **8th house**: This is the house of sex and death, which are deeply connected to the mystical quest and psychic ability.
- **9th House**: This is the house of philosophy and higher education, also travel.
- **10th House**: This house deals with career.
- **11th House**: This is the house of friendship but also hopes and fears, the ups and downs of fate, which is why Schon depicted the wheel of fortune.
- **12th House**: This is the house of the inner self and can show sorrows and limitations, like the person trapped in the stocks.

| | TABLE 5.3: **The Aspects, Their Distance, and Influence** | | |
|---|---|---|---|
| ☌ | **Conjunction** | 0° | positive or negative |
| ☍ | **Opposition** | 189° | negative |
| △ | **Trine** | 120° | positive |
| □ | **Square** | 90° | negative |
| ✳ | **Sextile** | 60° | positive |
| ∟ | **Semi-square** | 45° | negative |
| ⊼ | **Quincunx** | 150° | negative |
| ⊻ | **Semi-sextile** | 30° | positive |

Once the astrologer has gathered all of this information and placed the symbols for the signs and planets in the right places on the chart, he or she will look at how the planets relate to each other and how far apart they are from each other. The distance is measured in degrees and this relationship is called an aspect. Aspects add more information to the chart and need to be evaluated like the other parts. Table 5.3 shows the symbols for the eight aspects, the distance that they represent, and if they have a good or bad influence.

## Chinese Astrology

Although Western astrology stems from ancient Mesopotamia, other cultures around the world have observed the stars for omens and developed their own systems for interpreting them. The ancient Celts of the British Isles built a circle of massive stones called Stonehenge and used it to make predictions about celestial events. Likewise the Mayans of Central America created calendars that they used to make predictions. The most well known rival to the Western system, however, is the Chinese system.

In ancient China, diviners searched the sky for omens. By the Shang Dynasty (about 1766-1050 BCE) calendars were developed that could be used for divination for regular people. In the Chinese calendar there is a repeating cycle of 12 years and each of these 12 years has a different character named for an animal that symbolizes it. These 12 animal symbols are often called the Chinese zodiac but they should not be confused with the Western zodiac. The 12 Chinese signs do not relate to constellations and they have nothing to do with the ecliptic. The 12 signs are meant to describe the quality of a year and the nature of the people born in that year. When developing a chart for a person the signs can also be related to the month and the hour that the person is born. See Table 5.4 for the names and order of the Chinese signs and some of the years that they rule. To find other years just keep counting by 12 from the years that are shown. The colors of each sign are the ones associated with that sign. The traits given apply to any person born under that sign, regardless of the exact year.

TABLE 5.4: **The Chinese Zodiac**

|  | | | |
|---|---|---|---|
|  | | **Rat** | |
|  | 1972 | Charming | |
|  | 1984 | Fussy | |
|  | 1996 | & Frugal | |
|  | | **Ox** | |
|  | 1973 | Patient | |
|  | 1985 | Temperamental | |
|  | 1997 | & Stubborn | |
|  | | **Tiger** | |
|  | 1974 | Deep-thinking | |
|  | 1986 | Short-tempered | |
|  | 1998 | & Sympathetic | |
|  | | **Rabbit** | |
|  | 1975 | Talented | |
|  | 1987 | Trustworthy | |
|  | 1999 | & Ambitious | |

*(continues)*

TABLE 5.4: **The Chinese Zodiac** *(continued)*

| | |
|---|---|
|  | **Dragon**<br>1976 Energetic<br>1988 Short-tempered<br>2000 & Honest |
|  | **Snake**<br>1977 Deep<br>1989 Wise<br>2001 & Stingy |
| 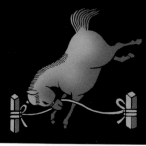 | **Horse**<br>1978 Complimentary<br>1990 Cheerful<br>2002 & Quick |
|  | **Sheep**<br>1979 Elegant<br>1991 Passionate<br>2003 & Shy |

TABLE 5.4: **The Chinese Zodiac**

| | |
|---|---|
| | **Monkey**<br>1980   Clever<br>1992   Inventive<br>2004   & Easily Discouraged |
| | **Cock**<br>1981   Devoted<br>1993   Eccentric<br>2005   & Untrusting |
| | **Dog**<br>1982   Loyal<br>1994   Honest<br>2006   & Critical |
| | **Boar**<br>1983   Gallant<br>1995   Idealistic<br>2007   & Disciplined |

# 6

# Divination Games

The Greek general Odysseus, also known by the Latin version of his name, Ulysses, was sailing home from the war in Troy when he landed on the island of Aeaea, where the beautiful but dangerous sorceress Circe was said to live. Odysseus landed with a group of about 40 men and decided to explore the island, but because of Circe's reputation he decided it would be wise to split the men into two groups and let one group go ahead first to see if things were safe.

Odysseus would head one group and he chose his most trusted companion, Eurylochus, to head the other group. But which group would go first? Odysseus decided to let the gods decide. He took off his bronze helmet, turned it upside down, and placed a white stone inside. Then Eurylochus found a darker stone of equal size to represent him and placed it in the helmet. Odysseus rolled the stones around in his helmet until one fell out. It was the dark stone, so Eurylochus took his men and marched ahead. Circe later turned Eurylochus and his men into pigs with a wave of her wand, but Odysseus was able to save them with the help of a magic herb.[22]

This story is derived from a scene in Homer's epic poem, the *Odyssey*. Although fictional, Homer's portrayal of how ancient Greek warriors used divination to make decisions is accurate.

## CASTING LOTS

In interpretative divination, instead of looking for omens in things that are already there, like dreams and nature, the diviner creates his or her own pattern to interpret. Ancient people believed that the gods or the divine powers wanted to communicate with them, and so when they used a device to create a random pattern there was really nothing random about it. It was an expression of divine will, and the seemingly chance pattern actually corresponded to events in their lives. This is another example of what Jung would call synchronicity.

Think of a war movie where the commander takes a handful of straws the same length but then breaks one shorter and hides it the bunch? Each solder then picks a straw from the commander's hand, and whoever gets the short straw has to go on a dangerous mission. This is an example of interpretive divination. Interpretative divination can also be used to get a yes or no answer. One of the simplest ways to do this is to flip a coin, something that has been around since ancient times. It is believed the first coins were stamped in the Greek kingdom of Lydia (modern-day Turkey) as early as about 600 BCE. Usually, the heads side of the coin is interpreted as yes and tails side means no, but the meaning can be alternated.

What did people do before the Lydians invented coins? They used sticks, rocks, bones, beans, or almost anything that worked. This type of divination can be found in any culture in the world and it comes under the general heading of casting lots. As we saw above, Greeks like Odysseus used lots in the form of stones to make decisions. Similarly, the commander in the war movie used straws as lots. And in chapter two, when Hippalus visited the oracle of Delphi, stone lots were used to determine the order of the questions. The Bible tells us that the ancient Hebrews also used lots to determine the will of God. There are numerous examples. In the book of Joshua, chapter seven, God commands Joshua to use lots to find a thief among his people. In the first book of Samuel, chapter 10, Saul is

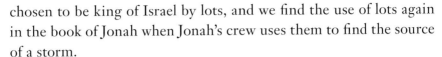

chosen to be king of Israel by lots, and we find the use of lots again in the book of Jonah when Jonah's crew uses them to find the source of a storm.

What did the ancient Hebrews actually use for lots? Several passages in the Bible mention two stones called **Urim and Thummim** that the priests of Israel used to divine the will of God. The trouble is that no one actually knows what Urim and Thummim were or how they were used. According to Jewish tradition, they were two stones set in a metal breastplate worn by the high priest. When the name of God was written on a piece of parchment and set behind the breastplate, the stones would glow and speak the word of God. Scholars tend to be a little skeptical about this explanation. It was more likely that Urim and Thummim were two stones that were used to obtain a yes or no answer, like flipping a coin. Some researchers, however, suggest that they were a series of 22 stones that had the letters of the Hebrew alphabet written one on each stone and were used to obtain more complex answers.

## RUNES

The Germanic peoples of Northern Europe also were known to use lots for divination. No one knows for sure what they used as lots, but ancient accounts mention glyphs or symbols that were carved in wood. Modern authors have tried to re-create their system by using the Germanic alphabets, which flourished from 150 to 700 and are known as *runes*. There are several runic alphabets falling into three main groups with variations in each group. Although their names can be translated, no one can be certain of their original divinatory meanings. Modern methods usually make use of a set of 24 runes, which are inscribed in clay, stone, or other materials and picked randomly from a bag or cast on a board with a pattern painted on it. Runes falling on different sections of the pattern would have different meanings or be applied to different parts of the question.

| TABLE 6.1: | **Viking Runes, as Described by Modern Author Ralph Blum**[23] | | |
|---|---|---|---|
| ᛗ | The Self | ᛃ | Harvest |
| ᚷ | Partnership | ᚲ | Opening |
| ᚠ | Signals | ↑ | Warrior |
| ᛟ | Retreat | ᛒ | Growth |
| ᚢ | Strength | ᛗ | Movement |
| ᚲ | Initiation | ᚱ | Flow |
| ᛉ | Constraint | ᚺ | Disruption |
| ᚷ | Fertility | ᚱ | Journey |
| ᛋ | Defense | ᚦ | Gateway |
| ᛣ | Protection | ᛉ | Breakthrough |
| ᚨ | Possessions | ᛁ | Standstill |
| ᚹ | Joy | ᛋ | Wholeness |

## DICE

Besides stones, one of the most common tools used for casting lots in the ancient world were bones. Especially popular were the small anklebones of an ox or sheep, which is called the *talus* in English and *astragalos* in Greek, but is popularly known as a knucklebone. Knucklebones have four sides and people would give each side a different meaning, which allowed for greater possibilities when used for divination. It also allowed them to be used for games of chance, something that seems to go hand in hand with divination in the ancient world.

Sometime in the ancient world people discovered that they could make little cubes out of bone, stone, wood, or clay, and number the sides with a series of dots. These are called dice and although they have six sides instead of four they quickly became interchangeable with

**Figure 6.1** *Ancient Greek knucklebone players.* (Werner Forman/Corbis)

knucklebones for games and divination. That is why divination with dice is called **astragalomancy**. The oldest known dice were found in what is now Iran, and they are part of a 5,000-year-old backgammon game. Since then, dice have been used for gambling and divination by the ancient Indians, Persians, Greeks, and Romans. Astragalomancy was popular in medieval Europe and continued to be practiced into the Renaissance, when it seems to have been replaced by divination with cards. Divination with dominos is also related. After all, dominos are like a cross between dice and cards.

To practice astragalomancy one simply has to assign a meaning for each of the 21 possible combinations that two dice can make, ask a question, throw the dice, and interpret the results. More complicated divination can be accomplished by using different shaped dice with more sides and different combinations of dice. To use dominos for astragalomancy, just turn them all upside down on the top of a table, swirl them around to shuffle, and then pick one.

## THE *I CHING*

It seems that all over Europe, India, and the Middle East people were casting lots. Anthropologists report that casting stones, sticks, shells, or bones were used for divination by tribal people in Africa, the South Pacific, the Americas, and other places. In China a different system emerged.

Archaeologists have determined that in prehistoric China, starting around 3000 BCE, the Chinese were divining by throwing animal bones into a fire and interpreting how they cracked. They mostly used the shoulder blades of large animals like cows, sheep, and deer, and because this bone is technically called the scapula this practice is called **scapulimancy**. These "oracle bones" are known about today, because the Chinese developed writing during the Shang Dynasty and they wrote a lot about them. Also, archaeologists have found more than 200,000 examples of actual oracle bones.

By 1050 BCE diviners started to realize that turtle shells were better for scapulimancy than bones because they were easier to prepare for the fire and the oval shape of the shell was like an idealized map of the world, called a ***mandala*** (Sanskrit for circle). Cracks in different areas on the shell could relate to the four directions of the earth: north, south, east, and west. Also around this time the Zhou or Chou rulers took over China and ruled until 256 BCE. Eventually in the Zhou period turtle shell divination was transformed into a divinatory book with 64 different symbols. each with its own meaning. The symbols are called **hexagrams** and look like stacks of six lines, some with gaps in the middle. To find the correct hexagram they used a complicated system involving dropping and picking up a set number of sticks cut from the stems of the yarrow herb.[24]

This book came to be called the *I Ching* (also spelled *Yi Jing, I Jing, Yi King,* or *Yi Ching,* and pronounced *EE jing*), which means the "Classic Book of Change." The *I Ching* is considered one of the five classic books of China and is highly valued for its philosophy as well as for its uses in divination. In Chinese tradition the *I Ching* is said to have been written by the legendary emperor Fu Hsi, who lived around 2800 BCE. He also supposedly invented writing, trapping, fishing, and cooking. Later the historic Zhou ruler King Wen (1099-1050 BCE) supposedly organized the 64 hexagrams and wrote a description of each. The *I Ching* also contains commentaries that are supposedly written by the famous Chinese philosopher, Confucius (551-479 BCE). Historians doubt that any of this is true, but the commentaries do express Confucian ideas even if they were not actually written by Confucius.

## THE PHILOSOPHY AND USE OF THE *I CHING*

The *I Ching* is not just a book of divination; it also is a classic of philosophy and magic. The symbols in the text are meant to express the creative forces of the universe and show 64 possible outcomes of their interaction. The Chinese, like a lot of other people, have observed

**Figure 6.2** *Chinese magical amulet with the* Tai Chi *and the eight trigrams.*

that there are two basic forces in the world that interact to create everything else. They call these forces **yin**, the feminine, and **yang**, the masculine. Yin and yang also relate to other pairs of opposites, like dark and light, night and day, rest and action, and most other pairs, except for good and evil. There is no negative value judgement here because both are good. The Chinese believe that evil arises from an imbalance of yin and yang and good from the proper balance.

Figure 6.3 shows a Chinese protective magical amulet that makes use of symbols related to the *I Ching*. The circle in the center with the *S* curve dividing it into blue and white is the *Tai Chi* or yin-yang symbol. It depicts the blue yin force and the white yang force continuously changing into one another. The eight symbols around the Tai Chi are each made of three lines called trigrams. The broken line with a gap in the center represents yin and the unbroken line represents yang. These trigrams are called "the eight precious things" and they represent the basic interactions of yin and yang spreading out to the eight directions of the world. Therefore, it is also another example of a mandala. All of the 64 hexagrams in the *I Ching* are made by combining these eight trigrams. Table 6.2 depicts each trigram with its name and other associations. Notice that in the amulet there are four trigrams of each sex, a mother, a father, three sons, and three daughters, and that the trigrams opposite each other are always of the opposite sex.

To create the 64 hexagrams any two trigrams can be combined with one on top and one on the bottom. When combined, the hexagram takes on a unique meaning beyond the two parts. For example, if we place the Gentle trigram above the Joyous, we get Figure 6.5, called Inner Truth. The space at the bottom of the Gentle has combined with the space at the top of the Joyous to form a useful looking inner space, suggesting the inner truth. The image also looked like a boat to the Chinese and that combined with the meaning of the trigrams, the

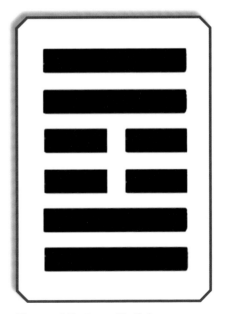

**Figure 6.3** *Inner Truth hexagram.*

*(text continues on page 92)*

TABLE 6.2: **The Eight Trigrams**

| | NAME | QUALITY | IMAGE | ROLE |
|---|---|---|---|---|
| | the Creative | Strong | Heaven | Father |
| | the Receptive | Yeilding | Earth | Mother |
| | the Arousing | Movement | Thunder | 1st Son |
| | the Abysmal | Dangerous | Water | 2nd Son |
| | Keeping Still | Resting | Mountain | 3rd Son |
| | the Gentle | Penetrating | Wind or Wood | 1st Daughter |
| | the Clinging | Light-giving | Fire | 2nd Daughter |
| | the Joyous | Joyful | Lake | 3rd Daughter |

## The Oldest Evidence of Divination

The oldest ceramics in the world are small prehistoric sculptures dug up at an archeological site in the modern Czech Republic. The most famous piece is a four-and-a-half-inch high abstract female nude known as the Venus of Dolni that was discovered in 1925 and was created between 29,000–25,000 BCE, in other words, up to 31,000 years ago. The Venus figure was made out of clay and thrown into a fire where it became hard and burned black.

People have found other prehistoric figures sculpted from clay and preserved because they were placed in caves, but before the Venus of Dolni and the related Czech finds it seems no one had ever thought of making the clay hard by firing it. But why did this prehistoric sculptor

**Figure 6.4** *The Venus of Dolni.* (Topham/The Image Works)

think of throwing the figure into the fire in the first place? No one can know for sure, but one theory that some archeologists propose is that throwing the figure into the fire was a type of divination. Perhaps, the artist wanted to see how the figure would react in the flames and

*(continues)*

*(continued)*

different reactions would have had different meanings, something like the Chinese method of divination in which they threw bones into a fire and interpreted the cracks that formed. Balls of clay might have been used first and then the figures were used to get a clearer message from or about that particular figure. If this is true, then these prehistoric figures are not only the oldest known ceramics but also the results of the oldest known divinatory practice and a type of interpretive divination.[27]

gentle wind or wood over the joyous lake, suggested a pleasant trip. So the commentary mentions things like, "Good Fortune. It furthers one to Cross a great water."[25] But it also applies this image to philosophical ideas about the inner truth. For example, true justice is based on finding the inner truth and having empathy with the people involved in a crime not just on getting revenge. This is a form of strength not weakness.[26] So you not only get some idea about where things are headed in your life but some wise advice from the Higher Self.

To consult the *I Ching* a good translation of the text is required. One of the most respected is the translation by Richard Wilhelm into German that was later translated into English by Cary F. Banes. This translation is the one that Jung studied and wrote an introduction for. To find answers to questions using the *I Ching* you will cast lots to get two hexagrams. For the lots you can use a complicated method involving 50 yarrow stalks but most people today prefer to use three coins. You can use Chinese coins, but any coins will do as long as you can tell heads from tails. You will throw the coins six times to find the lines for your hexagram, starting from the bottom up. There are four possible combinations as listed below:

1   Two tails and one head = a yang line in both hexagrams

2   Two heads and one tail = a yin line in both hexagrams

3   Three heads = a yang line in the first hexagram changing to a yin line in the second

4   Three tails = a yin line in the first hexagram changing to a yang line in the second

Of course, if you did not throw three of a kind for any of your throws and did not get a changing line you really only have one hexagram but most of the time you will have two. Now look up your first hexagram and read the commentary. Also pay attention to the commentaries for the changing lines. Now read the commentary for the second hexagram to see how the situation is changing. If you did not get a second hexagram then little will be changing and you have less to read. After completing this process, perhaps you not only will understand your situation better but will have some good ideas about what to do.

# 7

# The Tarot

Jane arrived at the front door of a tan house at the end of a suburban street and was welcomed in by Jill, the Tarot reader that several of her friends had recommended. Jill led her into the living room where she had a card table set up with two chairs set side by side. On the table there was a dark green tablecloth and spread out over the table a deck of beautifully illustrated cards with mysterious medieval-looking figures on them. The cards were laid down so that they faced the two chairs. On some of the cards there were figures that Jane recognized, such as Justice with her sword and scales, but there were others that she did not know, like the man hanging upside down by one foot. All of them excited her curiosity.

As this was Jane's first visit, Jill let her thumb through the cards as she explained to her that the best use of them was not to predict the future but to help her to understand her relationships with the people in her life and to get some wise advice from her inner guide, whom she called the Higher Self. Jill told her that when she needed to make decisions her Higher Self was always there to give sage advice, but the Higher Self preferred to communicate through symbols. Jill said, "The Tarot deck is a complete set of symbols and is therefore well-suited for this communication. There is nothing magic about it in itself; it is simply a tool that we can use for intuition."

Jill and Jane sat next to each other so they could both see the cards. Then Jill scooped up the cards and handed them to Jane to shuffle. While Jane was shuffling the cards, Jill prompted her to begin talking about what was bothering her. After a few complaints, Jill determined that Jane was having trouble with her husband and she needed some advice. Next, she had Jane cut the deck with her left hand, which symbolizes the unconscious. Jill took the three cards that were on the top of the pile that was left after the cut and laid them out left to right in a line. "These three represent you," she said.

She returned the block of cut cards to the deck and had Jane cut again. This time she skipped a space and laid out three more cards in a row to the right of the first three. "These represent your husband," she said. Then she repeated the process and laid the final three cards above the others in the center as if they were a bridge between the two sets. "And these represent your relationship," she said.

Before she even looked at the individual symbols on the cards, Jill looked at the direction of the figures as if they were characters in a story. She saw that most of the figures on Jane's cards were moving toward her husband's cards and that the figures on her husband's cards were moving toward Jane's. This was a good sign. Then she added the symbolism and began to see how Jane and her husband were relating or, at times, not relating because they had different goals. Jane was amazed at how accurately the cards described what she was feeling. She also realized that she would not have been able to put some of these feeling into words before this reading. Then Jill began to describe Jane's husband's cards and Jane got some insight into how her husband saw things. She felt that the cards were accurate but too diplomatic when it came to describing him. Last, Jill discussed the cards forming the relationship bridge, which pinpointed the disagreement. There were two knights, one for each of them and each with a different mission to accomplish, which symbolized Jane's and her husband's different goals. Between them was the seven of cups, which depicted a difficult choice and a lot of temptations.

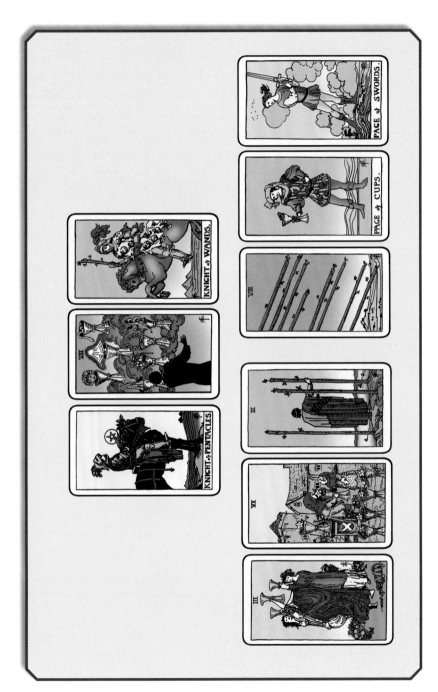

**Figure 7.1**  *Jill's Tarot layout for Jane and her husband, using the Waite-Smith Tarot.*  (Robert M. Place)

The finale came when Jill handed Jane the deck again and had her shuffle and cut to obtain advice from the Higher Self. These cards were laid on top of the ones that formed the bridge and showed Jane what she could do to make the relationship better, which involved a sensible compromise. Jane liked the advice but was not sure her husband would go along with it. "You can try," Jill said, "and if that doesn't work, why don't you come back with your husband and I will do both of you together?"

## DIVINATION WITH CARDS

The Tarot is covered last in this book for two reasons. First, of all of the forms of divination discussed here, the Tarot is one of the newest. Unlike palmistry, astrology, and the *I Ching*, it did not develop in the ancient past. It was created in the early 1400s in Renaissance Italy, which is old but not ancient. Occultists in the 1700s and 1800s, embarrassed that Tarot was so new, made up some phony histories for it. The most popular story was that it came from ancient Egypt, which is impossible because people in ancient Egypt did not have paper with which to make cards. Occultists did this because they saw that the Tarot, like the *I Ching*, is more than a tool for divination. They saw that it is a wise book of philosophy and magic that contains wisdom from the ancient world even though it was created in the Renaissance, and they wanted people to take it seriously.

The Tarot is called a book of philosophy, although it is actually a deck of cards with pictures, because it communicates with pictures the same way our Higher Self does, and when these symbolic pictures are viewed in sequence they express a mystical philosophy about the search for enlightenment. The Tarot communicates this philosophy like a book but with visual symbols instead of words, which raises the second reason it is covered last. Although the Tarot is a tool that is shuffled, cut, and laid down to get a divinatory answer and is, therefore, a type of interpretative divination, the answer is in pictures that take on a life of their own. So, the result is closer to intuitive divination, which comes back to dream divination discussed in Chapter One. A Tarot reading is like dreaming while awake and can be interpreted the same way.

Although the occultists appreciated the Tarot for its visual nature, some were uncomfortable with this open-ended interpretation and tried to find a secret formula for interpreting the cards. They said that each of the special 22 picture cards in the fifth suit were related to one of the 22 letters of the Hebrew alphabet and therefore also had astrological associations that were linked to the letters in the Kabalistic tradition. Various occultists tried several different ways to combine the cards and the Hebrew alphabet. A system like this may make interpretation easier for some, but the trouble is that none of these associations were intended by the artists who created the Tarot. The letters and astrological symbols do not have anything to do with the actual pictures on the cards. Also, the real power of the Tarot is that its pictures are not held down by a formula. They do have a history and contain symbolism, however, and the best way to learn more about the Tarot is to understand what these images meant to the people who made them. Let's look at what is in a Tarot deck.

## THE STRUCTURE OF THE TAROT

The Tarot is a deck of cards with five suits. Of the suits, four are related to a regular four-suit playing card deck, like those used to play poker or Go Fish. There are 10 cards in each of these suits that traditionally just showed a repetition of the suit symbol from ace to 10. These are called **pip** cards. Then there are some **royal cards** in each of these suits. In a Tarot there are four royal cards in each suit instead of three. There is a jack or page, a knight, a queen, and a king. Suit symbols are different than the hearts, diamonds, clubs, and spades used in playing cards, which will be explained later. Occultists liked to call these suits the *minor arcana*, which means the smaller secrets. The occultists were already suggesting that there was a secret code involved.

The thing that makes a Tarot deck different from a regular deck is that it also has a fifth suit with a parade of mystical figures on the cards. This is where the creators expressed the philosophy and this is the suit that the occultists called the *major arcana*, or the big secrets. Following is a list of these cards with their numbers in Roman numerals like the ones that appear on the cards in the traditional French version of the Tarot, called the Tarot of Marseilles. The Fool is a wild card and does not have a number.

The Fool

I. The *Bateleur* or The Magician

II. The *Papesse* or High Priestess

III. The Empress

IV. The Emperor

V. The Pope or *Hierophant*

VI. The Lovers

VII. The Chariot

VIII. Justice

IX. The Hermit

X. The Wheel of Fortune

XI. Force or Strength

XII. The Hanged Man

XIII. Death

XIV. Temperance

XV. The Devil

XVI. The Tower or Lightning

XVII. The Star

XVIII. The Moon

XIX.  The Sun

 XX.  Judgement or the Angel

XXI.  The World

## THE HISTORY OF THE TAROT

The first people to have cards of any kind were the Chinese, because they were the first to develop paper. They invented paper around the year 200 and first used it to make cards sometime between 300 and 1000. Cards were related to the creation of dominos, which probably came first. Early Chinese writers used the same name for dominos and cards. Cards were created primarily to play games of chance but they could also be used for divination. As the art of papermaking spread across Asia, various forms of card games developed as well as decks created solely for divination.

In the 1300s the Islamic people of the Middle East introduced a card deck to the Europeans. This deck, called the Mamluk deck, originated in Egypt in the 1200s and is named after the Islamic rulers of that time. The deck had four suits each with 10 pip cards and three all-male royal cards. It was a lot like a modern playing card deck except the suit symbols were cups, scimitars, coins, and polo sticks. The Europeans copied this deck and transformed it by changing the suits to cups, swords, coins, and staffs and at times adding a queen to the royal cards. As the deck spread through Europe, various countries changed the suit symbols, as shown in Table 7.1. Notice that the suits popular today in Britain and America originated in France. Although the other European countries changed the symbols on the cards, the Spanish and the Italians kept the original symbols. Sometime between 1410 and 1430 the Italians added a new fifth suit to this deck to create the Tarot.

The Tarot was created to play a particular card game that is the ancestor of the modern-day card game, bridge. The fifth suit was a natural **trump** suit that outranked the others, and each card in the suit outranked the one before it. These cards were modeled on a mystical parade in which each character in the parade trumped the one before. The parade was called a triumph and this is where the term trump comes from. In Italy, at first there were variations in the order and number of the these trumps, but after 1500 the French started making Tarot decks and they standardized the order to the one used in the Tarot of Marseilles. Although the Tarot was created for a game, all cards, including the four-suit decks, were also used for divination. Literary evidence attests that the four-suit decks were used for divination by the late 1400s and the Tarot by the early 1500s.[28]

The first occultist to write about the Tarot was the French author Courte de Gebelin (1719- or 1728-1784), who published his theories in his occult encyclopedia in 1781. He was the first to assert that the Tarot originated in ancient Egypt, that the fifth suit is related to the Hebrew alphabet and astrology, and that Gypsies had something to do with how the Tarot got to Europe. None of these things are true. De Gebelin, however, presented these ideas as theories, and he did not have as much historical information to work with as is available now. Thanks to de Gebelin, the Tarot became popular as a tool for divination and as a book of wisdom. The problem is that a lot of later authors repeated his theories as facts instead of looking at the information that historians were uncovering. In 1909 the occultist Arthur Edward Waite (1857-1942), who was a good enough historian to realize that the Tarot came from Renaissance Italy, hired another occultist, the gifted artist Pamela Colman Smith (1878-1946), to design a new deck that emphasized the mystical nature of the images instead of focusing on Hebrew letters. In this deck, which is now published as the Rider-Waite deck but is called the Waite-Smith deck by scholars, Smith added illustrations of people and things to the pip cards to make them easier to use for divination. She also related the four minor suits to four magical tools, to the four elements, and to divinatory qualities.

| TABLE 7.1: **A Chart of the Suit Symbols Adopted by Different European Countries** *(Illustrations by Robert M. Place)* | | | | |
|---|---|---|---|---|
| Italy | | | | |
| Spain | | | | |
| Switzerland | | | | |
| Germany | | | | |
| France & England | | | | |

1 **Cups**: water; intuition and emotions

2 **Swords**: air; thoughts and ideas

3 **Pentacles** (instead of coins): earth; physical senses, health, and wealth

4 **Wands** (instead of staffs): fire; feelings, work, and energy

The Waite-Smith deck has never been out of print. It is the most popular Tarot in the world today, and it is the deck that Jill was using in the opening story (see Figures 7.1 and 7.2).

## INTERPRETING THE TRUMPS

The meanings and connections with the four elements for the minor suits in the Waite-Smith Tarot seem to be similar to the interpretations that these suits would have had in the Renaissance. Only with Smith's illustrations it is easier to remember them. For the fifth suit, or major arcana, Smith's designs follow closely the images in the traditional Tarot of Marseilles but she made a few changes to adapt them to some occult ideas. For example, she kept the occultist's astrological connections for the trumps and because of that had Justice, traditionally number eight, change places with Strength, traditionally number 11, so they would correspond to the signs Libra and Leo in their order of correspondences.

When interpreting the trumps, however, it is best to understand as much as possible about the history and symbolism of each card and see them as the artists who created them in the 1400s saw them. All of the images in the Tarot can be found in other places in Renaissance art and the meaning of the cards can be compared with these images. Following is a brief description of the most likely Renaissance meaning for the major arcana.

The Tarot's fifth suit has an unnumbered Fool, which is a wild card that can be played instead of a trump, and 21 numbered trumps, which may have something to do with the 21 possible combinations of two dice. The 21 trumps can easily be divided into three groups of seven cards and when this is done each group has its own character. These three groups of seven, like other examples in Renaissance art, each relate to one of the three parts of the soul that the ancient philosopher Plato (429-347 BCE) talked about. It may seem odd that the soul has three parts and that Renaissance artists were concerned with this idea but a deeper look into this helps it make sense.

**Figure 7.2** *The Waite-Smith eight of cups, 1909 (left), compared to an early Italian eight of cups (1500).* (Robert M. Place)

Renaissance means rebirth, and this period was so named because the artists and writers of the Renaissance were trying to revive the art and philosophy of the ancient world. Plato was the most famous philosopher in the ancient world, so it is not surprising that Renaissance artists were interested in his ideas. One of the main themes in Plato's work was that humans have some conflicting ideas or desires. He found three main desires and called them the three parts of the soul:

1   **The soul of appetite**: The desire for material pleasures and things

2   **The soul of will**: The desire for fame and glory

3   **The soul of reason**: The desire for wisdom and spiritual insight

The three sections of the 21 trumps illustrate these three parts of the soul and as the soul parts move upward from the most selfish to the most unselfish and enlightened, so do the cards. This is a mystical ascent to greater wisdom and this is what makes the Tarot an excellent tool for communication with the Higher Self.

In illustrations 7.3 to 7.5 a Fool and the 21 trumps are rendered from various woodcut decks printed in Italy and France from the late 1400s to the 1700s. The trumps are divided into three groups of seven.

Figure 7.3 shows the Fool and the first seven trumps. The Fool is a traveling jester being attacked by a dog because he is a stranger. He is the outsider who will take this mystical journey through the three parts. The soul of appetite represents material desires like greed and lust and that is what we find here. The first trump in this section is the Magician, who is a street performer, the kind who cheats people out of money with his games of chance. The next four cards represent four rulers. There are four because this is the number associated with the physical world with its four directions, seasons, and elements. Notice that they are in male and female pairs: the Emperor and Empress, and the Pope and the female Pope or Papesse. These pairs are like the yin and yang symbols in the *I Ching*. All of these cards are trumped by the Lovers, which depict Cupid the god of lust. Below Cupid a young man

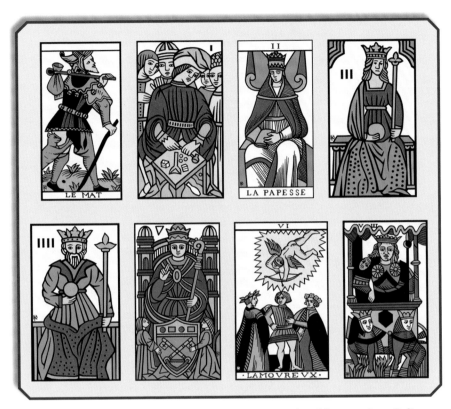

**Figure 7.3** *The Fool and the first seven trumps rendered from antique Italian and French decks. Clockwise from top, The Fool (French 1709), The Magician (Italian circa 1500), The Papesse (Italian 1780), The Empress (Italian circa 1500), The Emperor (Italian circa 1500), The Pope (Italian circa 1500), The Lovers (French 1650-1660), and The Chariot (French circa 1650).* (Robert M. Place)

is torn between his love for a woman with flowers in her hair, who represents sensuality, and a woman with a laurel wreath, who represents virtue. The Man chooses virtue and becomes the young warrior in the chariot in the last card, ready to move onto the soul of will.

Figure 7.4 depicts the cards representing the soul of will. The soul of will is the desire for fame and prestige that drives the hero to face death and hardship. Four of the cards in this section relate to death and hardship. The Hermit is an old man, who in the oldest decks was actually Father Time but by 1500 was replaced with the holy hermit, a spiritual hero who attains wisdom through self-denial or hardship. He faces the Wheel of Fortune, which depict the ups and down of fate and the foolishness of chasing worldly pleasures. A little further we find the Hanged Man, who is being punished by being hung by his foot. This was a punishment reserved for traitors. The next card is death, the Grim Reaper. However, by facing hardships and death the hero is also developing virtues. The other three cards spread through this

**Figure 7.4** *The second set of seven trumps rendered from antique Italian and French decks. Clockwise from top, Justice (Italian circa 1500), Hermit (Italian circa 1500), The Wheel of Fortune (Italian circa 1500), Strength (Italian circa 1500), The Hanged Man (French 1748), Death (Italian circa 1500), and Temperance (French circa 1650).* (Robert M. Place)

**Figure 7.5**   *The last seven trumps rendered from antique Italian and French decks. Clockwise from top, The Devil (Italian circa 1500), The Tower (French 1713), The Star (French 1713), The Moon (Italian circa 1500), The Sun (Italian circa 1500), Judgement (Italian circa 1500), and The World (French 1748).*   (Robert M. Place)

section depict three of the four **cardinal virtues** that Plato considered really important: Justice, Strength, and Temperance. The fourth cardinal virtue, Prudence, which was considered the most important, is discussed below.

Figure 7.5 depicts the last seven trumps that illustrate the soul of reason. Although the desire for fame seems heroic it is still a selfish desire, and in the soul of reason people aim for true balance and understanding. They no longer crave excessive pleasures or to prove themselves through suffering. This is the desire for the final virtue Prudence, which represents a higher state of wisdom. It might be surprising that this section starts with the Devil, the master of what is unreasonable. But to attain wisdom it is necessary to start by looking at the problem, selfishness or the devil. The next card shows a proud Tower, symbolizing egotism, getting blown away by a bolt of lightning. Then starts the climb up to heaven. In the sky on the Star card is the same ladder of seven planets that we saw in Figure 5.3. Although this ladder describes the descent of the soul into the body and is the basis of the horoscope, mystics also believed that they could ascend the

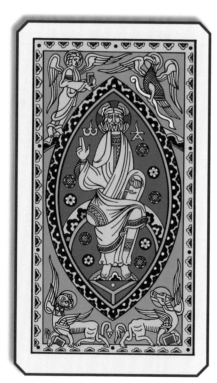

**Figure 7.6** *A rendering of the Christ in Majesty icon from the cover of a Medieval French Bible.* (Robert M. Place)

ladder while in a trance and reach heaven. The next two cards, the Moon and the Sun, are the heavenly rulers of the forces of yin and yang that rule the universe but we are going past even these regal figures. Judgement depicts an angel waking the dead on judgement day. It symbolizes the victory over death. And the final trump is a mandala, a sacred map of the world that depicts Prudence as a beautiful woman standing on the throne of God.[29]

To understand the World card it will be helpful to look at Figure 7.6, which shows a Christian holy image, or icon, of Christ sitting on his throne in heaven. Notice that Christ's throne is surrounded by four creatures: the lion, the bull, the eagle, and the angel. They are the same creatures that

## The Name of Pamela's Deck

When the Tarot deck that Arthur Edward Waite paid Pamela Colman Smith to create was first published by Rider in England, in December 1909, there were no other Tarot decks published in an English speaking country and it was simply called *Tarot Cards*. It was accompanied by Waite's book, *The Key to the Tarot*. The following year Waite added Smith's black and white drawings to the book and published it as *The Pictorial Key to the Tarot*. In 1971 an American publisher, U.S. Games, bought the right to publish the deck and published it

**Figure 7.7**  *Pamela Colman Smith, creator of the Waite-Smith tarot.*
(Robert M. Place)

under the title *The Rider Tarot Deck*. In later editions they changed the name to *Rider Tarot* and then *Rider-Waite Tarot*.[30]

Today most writers and scholars, in order to recognize Smith's contribution, refer to the deck as the *Waite-Smith Tarot*. By whatever name, it is still the most popular Tarot deck in the world. It is important to honor Smith as the designer. Some authors seem to be confused on this point and claim that Waite was the designer. But Waite could not draw and although he had some ideas about the symbolism of the Tarot that he no doubt shared with Pamela, she spent six months in her studio creating the illustrations and it is doubtful that Waite was hanging out there with her all of that time.[31]

surround Prudence on the World card. These creatures symbolize the four authors, or evangelists, who wrote the four gospels, which tell the story of Christ in the Bible. They are depicted spreading the word of Christ to the four corners of the world. Prudence, depicted in the Tarot as a beautiful woman, represents the wisdom that the evangelists are spreading, which is why she is standing on Christ's throne. In modern terms she may be thought of as the wisdom that comes from the Higher Self. In fact, the images in the Tarot are derived from the dreams and visions of mystics who were seeking this inner wisdom. They are actually illustrations of the archetypes that appear in our dreams, which brings us back to where we started. True divination is the attainment of this inner wisdom and the Tarot has all of the characters and symbols to illustrate the journey.

## DIVINATION PAST AND PRESENT

Divination has been practiced by humans since before the dawn of history. It has been practiced by every culture in the world. In the ancient cultures of Greece and Rome it was a respected part of their political and religious institutions and it influenced some of the most brilliant and influential minds in Western culture. Today the oracles of Greece are silent and the augurs of Rome are gone, but divination persists and is still a good way to develop intuition and to find out just how wise you really are deep inside.

The modern seeker may not be able to visit an oracle but there are still some ancient methods he or she can use. They include astrology, crystal gazing, and the ancient Chinese *I Ching*. There are also newer methods that still make use of ancient wisdom such as the Tarot and runes. And, perhaps the most ancient and yet the most available is your own dreams. It does not matter which method you use, the most important thing to remember is that the point of divination is not to predict the future but to get some wise advice from your Higher Self and use it to make some good decisions and create a better future.

# Timeline

**29,000–25,000 BCE**   The Venus of Dolni, possibly the oldest evidence of divination, was created

**3000 BCE**   The oldest known dice were created in ancient Iran, dice were used for both gaming and divination

The approximate date when the Indians developed palmistry

The approximate date when the Chinese began practicing divination by interpreting the cracks on shoulder blade bones thrown in a fire

**3rd millennium BCE**   The Hero Gilgamesh, who follows his dreams, is written about by the Sumerians

**2200 BCE**   The Sumerian king Gudea has his dream recorded

**2050–790 BCE**   The Egyptians create the first known dream books

**1792–1750 BCE**   The reign of Hammurabi, during which the first astrological texts were written

**1766–1050 BCE**   The Shang Dynasty in China in which the Chinese zodiac and divination with turtle shells developed

**1500–1000 BCE**   The Vedas, the sacred books of Hinduism, which contain dream divination, are written in India

**1500–400 BCE**   The Old Testament of the Bible is written by the Hebrews and contains accounts of prophecy, dream interpretation, and the casting of lots

**1050–256 BCE**   The Zhou or Chou Dynasty rules China and the *I Ching*, the Chinese classic of divination, is written

**1020 BCE**   *Chou Kung's Book of Auspicious and Inauspicious Dreams* is written in China

**900 BCE–393 CE** The oracle of Delphi operates in Greece

**605–562 BCE** The life of the Babylonian king, Nebuchadnezzar, who had his dream interpreted by Daniel

**600 BCE** Assyrians create the 12 signs of the zodiac and the first astrological natal charts

**Between 580 and 572 to between 500 and 490 BCE** The life of the Greek philosopher and mathematician Pythagoras, whose theories about the qualities of numbers become the basis for numerology

**500 BCE** Greeks begin to create dream books

**470-399 BCE** The life of Socrates, whom the oracle of Delphi declared "the wisest of men"

**300 BCE** Rome increases the number of augurs from three to nine

**1 CE** According to Christian legend, an omen called the Star of Bethlehem announces the birth of Christ, whose life was predicted by the Hebrew prophets

**146-170** Hellenistic astronomer and astrologer Claudius Ptolemy wrote during this period and creates his model of the cosmos

**150-200** The Germanic peoples of Northern Europe develop the runic alphabet, which was used for divination as well as magical inscriptions and calendars

**312** Roman emperor Constantine sees an omen of Christ's cross in the sky before the battle at Milvian Bridge

**373–414** The life of Synesius of Cyrene, a Greek Christian, who wrote a famous dream book

**832** Before an important battle with the English, the Scottish king Angus Mac Fergus sees an omen in the form of St. Andrew's cross in the sky

**1410–1430** The Tarot is created in Northern Italy

**1487** The *Mainz Fortune-telling Book* is published in Germany, the first book to mention divination with cards

**1501–1576** The life of Jerome Cardan, the astrologer and physician who developed a method of reading the lines on foreheads, called metoposcopy

**1555–1558**   French psychic and astrologer Nostradamus publishes his predictions

**1758–1828**   The life of German physician Franz Joseph Gall, who developed a method of reading the human skull called phrenology

**1778**   French occultist Courte de Gebelin publishes the first occult theories on the Tarot

**1909**   The Waite-Smith Tarot, the most famous modern Tarot, is published

**1914**   Psychoanalyst Carl G. Jung discovers synchronicity and develops a psychological explanation for how divination works

**1980s**   Several authors, including Ralph Blum and Stephen Flowers, develop a modern system of runic divination

# Glossary

**AILUROMANCY**  Divination by the observation of cats

**ARCHETYPE**  In Jungian psychology the name for separate personalities inside the unconscious that are the same in all people; in various mythologies, religions, and folk beliefs around the world they take the form of various heroes, gods, angels, and demons

**ASPECTS**  Astrological term for the relationships between planets in a horoscope, the relationships are measured in degrees

**ASTRAGALOMANCY**  Divination with dice or knucklebones of animals; the knucklebone or talus is called the astragalos in Greek

**ASTROLOGY**  The study of the relationship between the planets and constellations and human behavior and destiny

**AUGUR**  A priest of ancient Rome who looked to birds for signs of Jupiter's approval or disapproval

**AUTOMATIC WRITING**  Divination by putting a pen to paper and writing whatever comes to mind

**BIBLIOMANCY**  Divination by opening a book to a random page

**BRONTOSCOPY**  Divination by listening to thunder

**CARDINAL**  Astrological term for one of the three qualities of a sign; cardinal signs mark the change of one of the four seasons

**CARDINAL VIRTUE**  One of the four virtues—temperance, strength, justice, and prudence—that Plato considered essential to human development and that are depicted in the Tarot

**CHIROMANCY**  Another term for palm reading

**CLAIRVOYANCE**  The ability to know something without a physical connection to the source

CRYSTAL BALL   A ball made of a clear transparent rock called quartz, or a solid glass ball made to imitate quartz, used for scrying

DESCENDENT   Astrological term for the sign of the zodiac that is descending the horizon in the west at the moment of birth; one of the four angles

DIVINATION   Obtaining insight, wisdom, or direction from a source of wisdom in the unconscious known as the Higher Self

DREAM BOOK   A book that lists symbols found in dreams and their meanings

ECLIPTIC   The path the planets follow through the sky; a complete circle of 360 degrees that seems to surround the earth

ELEMENTS   In divination, a reference to the four ancient elements—earth, air, fire, and water—that are the four qualities applied to signs in astrology and related to the four minor suits in the Tarot

EPHEMERIS   A book used by astrologers listing the positions of the planets for each day of the year

FIXED   Astrological term for one of the three qualities of a sign; fixed signs are centered in one of the four seasons

FORTUNE-TELLING   Predicting the future; usually used to describe superstitious methods based on the belief that the future is fated and unchangeable

HARUSPICES   Ancient Roman diviners who read the livers of sacrificed animals; this type of divination is called *haruspicy*

HEXAGRAM   One of 64 symbols used in the *I Ching;* each has divinatory meaning and is composed of six lines, some with a break in the center, representing the yin or feminine force, and some unbroken, representing the yang or masculine force; the 64 hexagrams are composed of pairs of eight trigrams

HIGHER SELF   The unity of the conscious and unconscious minds and the source of inner wisdom

HIPPOMANCY   A form of divination practiced by ancient Celts in which divinatory meaning was obtained from the movements of sacred white horses

HOROSCOPE   An astrological birth or natal chart created for an individual, showing the positions of the planets and signs at the moment of birth

HOUSES   In astrology, the 12 divisions of the ecliptic that unlike the signs do not rotate; used as a measure of the movement of the signs and to add meaning to the position of each sign

HYDROMANCY   The use of a bowl or body of water for scrying

*I CHING*   An ancient Chinese book used for interpretive divination

INCUBATION   The process of focusing a dream to receive an answer to a specific question

INDUCTIVE DIVINATION   Looking for communication from the Higher Self in nature, such as through omens

INTERPRETATIVE DIVINATION   Creating a pattern with objects to communicate with the Higher Self, such as lots, dice, or tarot cards

INTUITIVE DIVINATION   Direct communication from the Higher Self, such as in a dream or vision

LOTS   The use of a tool such as sticks, rocks, bones, dice, or a coin, which is thrown on the ground or a table to gather information used in divination

LYCHNOMANCY   Divination performed by observing variations in the direction of a candle flame

MANDALA   An idealized or sacred map of the world, usually in a circular form; used as a board in divination or for symbolic significance as in the World card in the Tarot

METOPOSCOPY   Divination by reading the lines on the forehead

MIDHEAVEN   Astrological term for the sign of the zodiac that is at the top of the sky at the moment of birth; one of the four angles

MUTABLE   Astrological term for one of the three qualities of a sign; mutable signs are starting to change seasons

NADIR   Astrological term for the sign of the zodiac that is opposite the midheaven at the moment of birth; one of the four angles

NATAL ASTROLOGY   Astrology used to create charts for individuals based on the moment of their birth

ONEIROMANCY   Dream divination

ORACLE   A person who can communicate with a god, usually a woman; also the place where the communication happens

OUIJA BOARD   A board with the words *yes* and *no*, the letters of the alphabet, and the numbers 0-9 written on it; used with a pointer called a planchette to receive messages from the unconscious or the spirit world

PALMISTRY   Palm reading

PHRENOLOGY   Divination by reading the shape of the human skull and the bumps on the skull

PHYSIOGNOMY   An ancient Greek form of divination involving the shape of the human face

PIPS   The 10 numbered cards with a repetition of the suit symbol found in each suit of playing cards and in the four minor suits in the Tarot

PROPHECY   Predicting the future; particularly applied to diviners in the Bible

PYTHIA   The title of the oracle at Delphi, always a woman. Female oracles may also be referred to as sibyls

RISING SIGN   Astrological term for the sign of the zodiac that is coming over the horizon in the east at the moment of birth; one of the four angles

ROYAL CARDS   The jack, queen, and king in each suit of playing cards, and the jack or page, knight, queen, and king in the minor suits in the Tarot

RUNES   One of several Germanic alphabets, which flourished from 150 to 700; can be inscribed on clay, wood, or stone pieces to be used as lots

SCAPULIMANCY   The use of the shoulder blades or scapulas of large animals, like cows, sheep, and deer, which are thrown into a fire to crack and are then interpreted as a form of divination; particularly in ancient China

SCRYING   Looking for a vision in a transparent or shiny surface, such as a bowl of water, a mirror, or a crystal ball

SYNCHRONICITY   Jung's term for an event in physical reality that coincides with a psychological event in a way that is meaningful and yet without a cause and effect relationship

TAROT   A deck of 78 cards used in divination composed of five suits: four minor suits that are similar to regular playing cards, and a fifth suit with 22 mystical figures

TASSEOMANCY   Divination by reading tea leaves, coffee grounds, or wine residue that are left in a cup after drinking

TELEPATHY   Receiving information from mind to mind without using the five senses

TRUMPS   The 21 numbered cards that along with the Fool comprise the fifth suit in the Tarot

UNCONSCIOUS   The largest part of the mind; the part of the mind that is not conscious but is the source of all dreams, memories, and thoughts

URIM AND THUMMIM   Divinatory stones or lots used by ancient Hebrew priests

YANG   In Chinese philosophy the masculine, light, warm, active force

YIN   In Chinese philosophy the feminine, dark, cool, passive force

ZODIAC   The 12 astrological signs that each take up 30 degrees on the circle of the ecliptic, which is the path that the planets follow through the sky: it can also refer to the 12 constellations found along the ecliptic

# Endnotes

1 C. G. Jung, *Psychology and the Occult*, Hull, Trans. (Princeton: Princeton University Press, 1977), 135.

2 C. G. Jung and Aniela Jaffe, ed., *Memories, Dreams, Reflections* (New York: Vintage Books, 1989), 183.

3 Robert L. Van de Castle, *Our Dreaming Mind* (New York: Ballantine Books, 1994), 23–22.

4 Ibid., 84.

5 Ibid., 62.

6 Simon Hornblower and Anthony Spawforth, eds., *The Oxford Classical Dictionary*. 3d ed. (Oxford: Oxford University Press, 1996), 445.

7 John Hale, "The Delphic Oracle: interview with Rachel Kohn." *The Ark*, Radio National, August 8, 2004. Available online. URL: http://www.abc.net.au/rn/relig/ark/stories/s1266794.htm.

8 Hornblower and Spawforth, *The Oxford Classical Dictionary*. 3d ed., 1071.

9 "Themistocles," History.com Encyclopedia. Available online. URL: http://www.history.com/encyclopedia.do?articleId=223985.

10 Andrew Lang, *Crystal Visions, Savage and Civilised* (London: Longmans, Green, and Co., 1900), 83.

11 Lewis Spence, *An Encyclopedia of Occultism* (New York: Dover, 2003), 95.

12 Emile Grillot De Givry, *Picture Museum of Sorcery, Magic, and Alchemy*, Locke, trans. (New York: University Books, 1963), 304–306.

13 Rosemary Ellen Guiley, *Harper's Encyclopedia of Mystical & Paranormal Experience* (San Francisco: HarperCollins, 1991), 534.

14 Ibid., 553.

15 Nostradamus, "Letters," Peter Lemesurier, trans. Available online. URL: http://www.prophe ties.it/nostradamus/inedites/inedites3.htm (Accessed September 4, 2007).

16 Guiley, *Harper's Encyclopedia of Mystical & Paranormal Experience*, 407–409.

17 William Smith, ed., "Augur, Augurium," from *A Dictionary of Greek and Roman Antiquities* (London, UK: John Murray, 1875), 175.

18 David Pickering, *Cassell's Dictionary of Superstitions* (New York: Sterling, 1995), 107.

19 Martin Li, *Adventure Guide to Scotland* (Walpole, Mass.: Hunter Publishing, 2005), 16.

20 Ann Fiery, *The Book of Divination* (San Francisco: Chronicle Books, 1999), 55.

21  David Wray, "Astrology in Ancient Rome: Poetry, Prophecy and Power," Talk delivered at the University of Chicago Humanities Open House, October 27, 2001. Available online. URL: http://fathom.lib.uchicago.edu/1/777777122543/.

22  Homer, *The Odyssey*, Translated by W. H. D. Rouse, trans. (New York: Mentor Books, 1961), 109.

23  Ralph Blum, *The Book of Runes* (New York: St. Martin's Press, 1982).

24  S. J. Marshall, *The Mandate of Heaven: Hidden History in the I-Ching* (New York: Columbia University Press, 2001), 12–16.

25  Richard Wilhelm, *The I Ching or Book of Changes*, Cary F. Banes,

trans. (New York: Princeton University Press, 1978), 235.

26  Ibid., 236.

27  Heather Pringle, "New Women of the Ice Age," *Discover Magazine* 4, April 1998.

28  Robert M. Place, *The Tarot: History, Symbolism, and Divination* (New York: Tarcher/Penguin, 2005), 9–27.

29  Ibid., 127–169.

30  Frank K. Jensen, *The Story of the Waite-Smith Tarot* (Croydon Hills, Australia: Association for Tarot Studies, 2006), 137–141.

31  Place, *The Tarot: History, Symbolism, and Divination*, 182–186.

# Further Resources

## Jungian Psychology

Jung, Carl G. *Man and His Symbols*. New York: Doubleday, 1964.

Jung, C. G. *Memories, Dreams, Reflections*. Edited by Aniela Jaffe. New York: Vintage Books, 1989.

## Intuitive Divination

Guiley, Rosemary Ellen. *Dreamwork for the Soul*. New York: Berkley Books, 1998.

Guiley, Rosemary Ellen. *The Encyclopedia of Dreams: Symbols and Interpretations*. New York: Crossroad, 1993.

Hogue, John. *Nostradamus: The Complete Prophecies*. Shafesbury, Dorset: Element, 1997.

Lang, Andrew. *Crystal Visions, Savage and Civilised*. London, UK: Longmans, Green, and Co., 1900.

Secheist, Elsie. *Edgar Cayce Dreams: Your Magic Mirror*. New York: Warner Books, 1968.

Van de Castle, Robert L. *Our Dreaming Mind*. New York: Ballantine, 1994.

## Inductive Divination

Chiba, Reiko. *The Japanese Fortune Calendar*. North Clarendon, Vt.: Tuttle Publishing, 1991.

Hoffman, Enid. *Hands: A Complete Guide to Palmistry*. Atglen, Pa.: Whitford Press, 1983.

Innes, Brian. *Horoscopes: How to Draw and Interpret Them*. New York: Crescent Books, 1976.

Kenton, Warren. *Astrology: The Celestial Mirror*. New York: Thames and Hudson, 1974.

Schimmel, Annemarie. *The Mystery of Numbers*. New York: Oxford University
Press, 1993.

Woolfolk, Joanna Martine. *The Only Astrology Book You'll Ever Need*. Lanham, Md.:
Scarborough House, 1990.

## Interpretative Divination

Blum, Ralph. *The Book of Runes*. New York: St. Martin's Press, 1982.

Jensen, Frank K. *The Story of the Waite-Smith Tarot*. Croydon Hills, Australia:
Association for Tarot Studies, 2006.

Kaplan, Stuart R. *The Encyclopedia of the Tarot, Vol. I, and Vol II*. New York: U.S.
Games, 1978, 1986.

Marshall, S. J. *The Mandate of Heaven: Hidden History in the I-Ching*. New York:
Columbia University Press, 2001.

Moakley, Gertrude. *The Tarot Cards Painted by Bonifacio Bembo*. New York: The
New York Public Library, 1966.

Pennick, Nigel. *Games of the God: the Origin of Board Games in Magic and Divination*.
York Beach, Maine: Samuel Weiser, 1989.

Place, Robert M. *The Buddha Tarot Companion Book: A Mandala of Cards*. St. Paul:
Llewellyn Publications, 2004.

Place, Robert M. *The Tarot: History, Symbolism, and Divination*. New York: Tarcher/
Penguin, 2005.

Waite, Arthur Edward. *The Pictorial Key to the Tarot*. New York: Harper and Row,
1971.

Wilhelm, Richard. *The I Ching or Book of Changes*. Translated by Cary F. Banes.
New York: Princeton University Press, 1978.

## General

Astrop, John. *Secrets of Divination*. London, UK: DK Publishing, 2001.

De Givry, Emile Grillot. *Picture Museum of Sorcery, Magic, and Alchemy*. Translated
by Courtenay Locke. New York: University Books, 1963.

DuQuette, Lon Milo. *The Book of Ordinary Oracles*. Boston: Wiser Books, 2005.

Fiery, Ann. *The Book of Divination*. San Francisco: Chronicle Books, 1999.

Guiley, Rosemary Ellen. *Harper's Encyclopedia of Mystical & Paranormal Experience*.
San Francisco: HarperCollins, 1991.

# Bibliography

Homer. *The Odyssey*. Translated by W. H. D. Rouse. New York: Mentor Books, 1961.

Hornblower, Simon, and Anthony Spawforth, eds. *The Oxford Classical Dictionary*. 3d ed. Oxford: Oxford University Press, 1996, 445.

Jung, C. G. *Psychology and the Occult*. Translated by R. F. C. Hull. Princeton: Princeton University Press, 1977.

Li, Martin. *Adventure Guide to Scotland*. Walpole, Mass.: Hunter Publishing, 2005.

Pickering, David. *Cassell's Dictionary of Superstitions*. New York: Sterling, 1995.

Pringle, Heather. "New Women of the Ice Age," *Discover Magazine* 4 (April 1998).

Smith, William, ed. "Augur, Augurium," in *A Dictionary of Greek and Roman Antiquities*. London, UK: John Murray, 1875.

Spence, Lewis. *An Encyclopedia of Occultism*. New York: Dover, 2003.

# Index

**A**

ailuromancy, 52, 117
alphabets, Germanic, 83
amulet, Chinese magical, *88*
Angus Mac Fergus, 51
Apollo, 31, 33, 36
Aquarius, 73
archaeology, 36, 86
archetypes, 18, 117
Aries, 71
Asclepius, 28
aspects, 70, 75, 117
astragalomancy, 86, 117
astrology, 61–79, 117
    ancient Greece, 65–66
    ancient Rome, 61–63
    China, 76–79
    horoscopes, 66–79
    Mesopotamia, 64–65
    star charts, 63–66
augurs, 47, 117
Augustus (Roman emperor), *61,*
  *63*
automatic writing, 38, 117

**B**

Babylonians, ancient, 37, 41
Banes, Cary F., 92
Bible, 26–27

bibliomancy, 51, 117
Blum, Ralph, 84
Boar (in Chinese zodiac), 79
brontoscopy, 50, 117

**C**

Cancer (zodiac sign), 71
*The Canterbury Tales* (Chaucer),
  44
Capricorn, 73
Cardan, Jerome, 52, 54
card games, 101
cardinal (term), 117
cardinal virtue, 117
casting lots
    divination by, 82–83
    *I Ching*, 92–93
Celts, 44
Chariot (Tarot trump), 107
Chaucer, Geoffrey, 44
China, astrology in, 76–79
Chinese magical amulet, *88*
chiromancy, 117. *See also*
  palmistry
*Chou Kung's Book of Auspicious and*
  *Inauspicious Dreams*, 25
Christian iconography, 110, 112
Christianity, 27, 37, 51
Christ in Majesty icon, *110*

clairvoyance, 14, 117
Cock (in Chinese zodiac), 79
coins, flipping, 82
collective unconscious, 18
comets, 50
common objects, omens in,
   51–52
Confucius, 87
Conjunction (aspect), 75
Constantine (Roman emperor),
   50–51
constellations, 63
Copernicus, Nicolaus, 64
crystal ball, 40, *40*, 45, 118
cuneiform, *23*, 24
Cups (Tarot), 104

**D**

Daniel (Hebrew prophet), 26
Death (Tarot trump), 108
Dee, John, 45
descendent (term), 70, 118
Devil (Tarot trump), 110
dice, divination by, 85–86
divination, 81–93, 118
   ancient Greece, 81, 82
   by casting lots, 82–83
   by dice, 85–86
   by dreams, 22–25
   by *I Ching*, 86–90, 92–93
   prehistoric, 91–92
   by runes, 83–84
Dog (in Chinese zodiac), 79
Dragon (in Chinese zodiac),
   78
dream(s), 21–25
   divination by, 22–25
   of Carl Jung, 19

dream books, 25–29, 118
   ancient civilizations, 25
   Bible, 26–27
   *Chou Kung's Book of Auspicious*
      *and Inauspicious Dreams*, 25
   *I Ching*, 25
   *Treatise on the Soul* (Tertullian),
      27
   Vedas, 25

**E**

eclipses, 50
ecliptic, 64, 118
Egypt, oracles in ancient, 37
elements, 70, 118
Elizabeth I (queen of England), 38
Emperor/Empress (Tarot trump),
   106
ephemeris, 66, 118
ethylene gas, 36

**F**

*The Faerie Queene* (Spenser), 44
finger shapes, 54
fixed (term), 118
Fool (Tarot), 106
forehead lines, *53*
fortune-telling, 118
Freud, Sigmund, 27–28
Fu Hsi (legendary Chinese
   emperor), 87
*fuji* (Chinese oracle board), 38

**G**

Gall, Franz Joseph, 52
Gebelin, Courte de, 102
Gemini, 71
Germanic alphabets, 83

Gilgamesh, 24–25
Greece, ancient
    astrology, 65–66
    divination, 81, 82
    oracles, 31–37
Gudea (king of Sumeria), 24

**H**

Hammurabi (king of Babylonia), 64
hand, minor marks of the, 57
hand shape, 54
Hanged Man (Tarot trump), 108
haruspices, 51, 118
Hebrew alphabet, 99
Hebrew oracles, 37
Hermit (Tarot trump), 107–108
Herodotus, 37
hexagram, 87, 118
Higher Self, 18, 112, 118
hippomancy, 52, 118
horoscope(s), 66–79, 119
    aspects, 75
    Chinese zodiac, 77–79
    planets, 69
    by Erhard S. Schon, 67
    signs of the zodiac, 71–73
Horse (in Chinese zodiac), 78
houses (of zodiac), 68, 74, 119
human body, omens in, 52–58
hydromancy, 41, 119

**I**

I Ching, 16, 87, 119
    casting lots, 92–93
    divination by, 86–90, 92–93
    dream book, 25
    philosophy, 87–88

incubation, 28, 119
inductive divination, 20, 119
interpretative divination, 20, 119
intuitive divination, 20, 119
Islam, 101

**J**

Joseph (Hebrew prophet), 26–27
Julius Caesar (Roman emperor), 61
Jung, Carl G., 14–19, 15, 29
Jupiter, 69
Justice (Tarot trump), 109

**K**

The Key to the Tarot (Waite), 111
knucklebones, 85, 85

**L**

Leo, 72
Libra, 72
lightning, 50
lots, 32, 119
Lovers (Tarot trump), 106
Luther, Martin, 27
Lydia (Greek kingdom), 82
lynchnomancy, 52, 119

**M**

Magician (Tarot trump), 106
major arcana (big secrets), 100
Mamluk deck (cards), 101
mandala, 87, 119
Mars, 69
Mercury, 69
Mesopotamia, astrology in, 64–65
Metoposcopia (Cardan), 53
metoposcopy, 52, 119

midheaven, 70, 119
Milvian Bridge, Battle of, 51
*minor arcana* (smaller secrets), 99
minor marks of the hand, 57
mirror, 43–44
Mohammad, 27
Monkey (in Chinese zodiac), 79
Moon (as planet), 69
Moon (Tarot trump), 110
mutable (term), 119

**N**

nadir, 70, 119
natal astrology, 120
natal chart, 65
Native American tribes, 41
Nebuchadnezzar (king of Babylo-
    nia), 26
Neptune, 69
Nostradamus, Michel, 42–43
numbers, as omens, 59–60
numerology, 59–60

**O**

Octavian (Roman emperor),
    61–63
Odysseus, 81
*Odyssey* (Homer), 81
omens, 47–60
    ancient Rome, 47–51
    in common objects, 51–52
    in human body, 52–58
    numbers as, 59–60
    in sky, 49–51
oneiromancy, 23, 120
Opposition (aspect), 75
oracle(s), 31–38, 120
    ancient Egypt, 37
    ancient Greece, 31–37

Babylonia, 37
    Hebrew, 37
oracle bones, 86
Ouija board, 38, 120
Ox (in Chinese zodiac), 77

**P**

palmistry, 52–58, 120
palm lines, 54–56, *55*
palm mounds, 56, *58*
papermaking, 101
Pentacles (Tarot), 104
Philemon, 19
philosophy
    *I Ching*, 87–88
    Tarot, 98
phrenology, 52, 120
physiognomy, 52, 120
*The Pictorial Key to the Tarot*
    (Waite), 111
pips, 99, 120
Pisces, 73
*planchette*, 38
planets, 64, *66*, 68, 69
Plato, 105, 106
Pluto, 69
Pope/Papesse (Tarot trump), 106
prehistoric divination, 91–92
priestess at Delphi, *32*
*The Prophecies* (Nostradamus),
    42–43
prophecy, 23, 120
Prudence (Tarot trump), 109, 110,
    112
Ptolemy, 65–66
Ptolemy's ladder of the planets,
    *66*
Pythagoras, 59
pythia, 32, 33, 120

### Q

Quincunx (aspect), 75

### R

Rabbit (in Chinese zodiac), 77
Rat (in Chinese zodiac), 77
Renaissance, 98, 105
Rider-Waite Tarot, 102, 111
rising sign, 70, 120
Rome, ancient
    astrology, 61–63
    omens, 47–51
royal cards, 99, 120
runes, 120
    divination by, 83–84
    Viking, 84

### S

Sagittarius, 73
Saturn, 69
scapulimancy, 86, 120
Schon, Erhard S., 68
Scorpio, 72
scrying, 40–45, 121
Semi-sextile (aspect), 75
Semi-square (aspect), 75
Sextile (aspect), 75
Shang Dynasty, 76, 86
Sheep (in Chinese zodiac), 78
signs, qualities of, 70
sky, omens in the, 49–51
Smith, Pamela Colman, 102, 111
Smith-Waite deck (Tarot cards), 102
Snake (in Chinese zodiac), 78
*Snow White* (fairy tale), 44
Sophocles, 36
soul, parts of, 105–106
Spenser, Edmund, 44

Square (aspect), 75
Star (Tarot trump), 110
star charts, 63–66
Star of Bethlehem, 50
stars, 50
stones, polished, 44
straws, picking, 82
Strength (Tarot trump), 109
suit symbols, Tarot, 103
Sun (as planet), 69
Sun (Tarot trump), 110
superstitions, 49
Swords (Tarot), 104
symbolism, of Tarot, 104–112
synchronicity, 15, 121
Synesius of Cyrene, 27

### T

*Tai Chi*, 89
Tarot, 95–112, 121
    history of, 98, 101–104
    interpretation of, 104–112
    layout of, 97
    philosophy, 98
    structure of, 99–101
    symbolism of, 104–112
Tarot of Marseilles, 102, 104
tasseomancy, 52, 121
Taurus, 71
telepathy, 14, 121
Temperance (Tarot trump), 109
Tertullian, 27
*Tetrabiblios* (Ptolemy), 65
Themistocles, 34
thunder, 50
Tiger (in Chinese zodiac), 77
Tower (Tarot trump), 110
*Treatise on the Soul* (Tertullian), 27
trigrams, 89–90

Trine (aspect), 75
trumps, 102, *107–109*, 121

### U

unconscious, 16–18, 121
Uranus, 69
Urim and Thummim, 83, 121

### V

Vedas, 25
Venus (planet), 69
Venus of Dolni, *91*
Viking runes, 84
Virgo, 72
visions, 39–45. *See also* scrying

### W

Waite, Arthur Edward, 102, 111
Waite-Smith Tarot, *105*, 111

Wands (Tarot), 104
Wen (Chinese king), 87
Wheel of Fortune (Tarot trump),
    108
Wilhelm, Richard, 92
*The Wizard of Oz* (Film), 41
writing, automatic, 38, 117

### X

Xerxes (emperor of Persia), 34

### Y

yang, 88, 121
yin, 88, 121

### Z

Zhou Dynasty, 87
zodiac, 64, 121

# About the Author

ROBERT M. PLACE is an author and a visionary artist and illustrator, whose award-winning works in painting and sculpture have been displayed in galleries and museums in America, Europe, and Japan and graced the covers and pages of numerous books and publications. He is the designer, illustrator, and co-author, with Rosemary Ellen Guiley, of: *The Alchemical Tarot* and *The Angels Tarot*. He is the designer, illustrator, and author of *The Buddha Tarot*, *The Tarot of the Saints*, and *The Vampire Tarot*. He is the author of *The Buddha Tarot Companion*, and *The Tarot: History, Symbolism, and Divination*, which Booklist has said, "may be the best book ever written on... the tarot." For *Mysteries, Legends, and Unexplained Phenomena* he has also authored *Shamanism* and is the cover illustrator for the series.

# About the Consulting Editor

ROSEMARY ELLEN GUILEY is one of the foremost authorities on the paranormal. Psychic experiences in childhood led to her lifelong study and research of paranormal mysteries. A journalist by training, she has worked full time in the paranormal since 1983, as an author, presenter, and investigator. She has written 31 nonfiction books on paranormal topics, translated into 13 languages, and hundreds of articles. She has experienced many of the phenomena she has researched. She has appeared on numerous television, documentary, and radio shows. She is also a member of the League of Paranormal Gentlemen for Spooked Productions, a columnist for *TAPS Paramagazine*, a consulting editor for *FATE* magazine, and a writer for the "Paranormal Insider" blog. Ms. Guiley's books include *The Encyclopedia of Angels*, *The Encyclopedia of Magic and Alchemy*, *The Encyclopedia of Saints*, *The Encyclopedia of Vampires, Werewolves, and Other Monsters*, and *The Encyclopedia of Witches and Witchcraft*, all from Facts On File. She lives in Maryland and her Web site is http://www.visionaryliving.com.